W0008887

Connemara
after the
Famine

Connemara after the Famine

JOURNAL OF A SURVEY OF
THE MARTIN ESTATE BY THOMAS
COLVILLE SCOTT, 1853

Edited & Introduced by Tim Robinson

THE LILLIPUT PRESS : 1995

First published in 1995 by
THE LILLIPUT PRESS LIMITED
4 Rosemount Terrace, Arbour Hill,
Dublin 7, Ireland.

A CIP record for this
title is available from
The British Library.

ISBN 1 874675 69 4

Cover design by Jarlath Hayes
Set in 12.5 on 16 Monotype Centaur by
Printed in England by
Cambridge University Press

Contents

INTRODUCTION
by Tim Robinson

In August of 1849, at the Mart in London, a huge property was put up for auction: the Martin estate in the west of Ireland. The vendors were at a loss for words to describe its attractions:

Any description which can be written would fall short of the advantages which would present themselves to the eye of an intelligent person, in his survey of this truly wonderful district. It is impossible for the mind of man to conceive anything necessary but capital, and a judicious application of it, for rendering this vast Property fertile beyond a parallel that this Estate does not contain within itself; facilities for Draining, the formation of Roads, inland Navigation, abundance of lime, sea-weed for manure, valuable kelp shores, innumerable beautiful sites for Buildings, and the soil generally might be designated, to use a homely phrase, as one vast dung-heap...*

The estate, of 196,540 acres, comprised most of the territory stretching westwards from the town of Galway and known as Connemara. The detailed description of it in the sales prospectus was in terms of about two hundred of the basic land-divisions known

---

* 'Particulars of Sale of the Galway Estates of the Late Thomas Barnewall Martin, Esq.' (London 1849).

as townlands, and this was to be read in the light of the following special inducement to buy:

The number of Tenants on each Townland, and the amounts of their Rents, have been taken from a Survey, and ascertained Rental in the year 1847, but many changes advantageous to a Purchaser have since taken place, and the same Tenants by name, and in number, will not now be found on the Lands.

That year of 1847 had been the worst of several consecutive years of famine, and it was to be understood that those missing tenants had abandoned their holdings to crowd into the work-houses or the emigrant ships to the New World, or they were dead; in any case they no longer infested the ground, which was left as a blank canvas on which Capital could paint a fair and profitable landscape.

Topographically Connemara appears as a natural refuge, or as a trap. The twenty-four-mile length of Lough Corrib fences it off on the east, and the Atlantic provides the rest of its bounds: a low and labyrinthine shoreline along the south, westward-thrusting reefs and promontories, and across the north, a sea inlet almost compa-rable with a Norwegian fiord, Killary Harbour. Steep mountains rising to over two thousand feet occupy most of the northern half of this isolated region, much of the south is a sea-level plain intri-cately interrupted by some two hundred lakes, and both highlands and lowlands are blanketed with bog, up to ten or fifteen feet deep in places and fed by a copiously oceanic sky. In early historic times (but history only made brief and tentative incursions here until much later) most of this territory was held by a people known as the Conmaicne Mara, the Conmaicne of the Sea; they counted their descent from a Celtic hero, Conmac the son of Maeve and Fergus, but they played no great role in memorable matters, and the name 'Connemara' is almost the only trace of their former presence. In the early thirteenth century they were eclipsed by the O'Flahertys, who had been masters of the fertile plain stretching eastwards from Lough Corrib, until they were driven across the lough by the Normans. Thereafter, for three hundred years, the O'Flahertys ruled and feuded in their obscure hinterlands according to the old Gaelic customs, while Galway, controlling the isthmus between Lough Corrib and the bay, grew into a walled city, sea-linked to Renaissance ways and ruled by an oligarchy of merchant and banking families of Norman origin, among whom the Martins were prominent. The disaffected and rebellious O'Flahertys were the natural enemies of the Galway merchants, who, it is said, had the legend 'From the ferocious O'Flahertys, O Lord deliver us' inscribed over the west gate of their loyal and industrious little polity. But the Martins learned to deal with the O'Flahertys, and bought some land near town from them, and later obliged them with mortgages on other bits of land further out, which in due course were forfeited and became part of the Martin holdings. Deep in Connemara one of the O'Flaherty strongholds was Baile na hInse, 'the settlement of the island', so called because it was centred on a lake-island castle. When Queen Elizabeth's statesmen succeeded in partially netting the O'Flahertys in the web of feudal duties and prerogatives radiating from the English throne, the western half of Connemara became the Barony of Ballynahinch, by anglicization of the Irish name of this settlement. Ballynahinch was to become the heart of the Martin estate in later times.

The remorseless rending of Europe between two faiths eventually brought the Galway townfolk and the O'Flahertys into alliance in the 1640s. Both supported the Catholic Confederation in the Irish rebellion that budded off from the Civil War in England; both suffered for it when Protestant Parliament overthrew Catholic King, and Cromwell's army savaged Ireland. One O'Flaherty chief was hanged and the rest expropriated, and their countless acres of wasteland were distributed to Cromwell's financial backers and to Catholic landowners dispossessed of better lands now reserved for Protestants. The Martins lost some Galway property and were given large tracts of Connemara, and soon added to them some holdings the Cromwellian grantees were happy to sell off. Not for nothing was the head of the Martin family a lawyer known as Nimble Dick; by adroit self-representation as a friend to both sides, he was restored to some of his old holdings, and later had his ownership of the new ones confirmed by King William. Thus the Martins bobbed to the surface, after fifty years of religious strife, as the largest landowners in either Britain or Ireland.

The next generation of Martins built a mansion on the lakeshore near the ruined O'Flaherty castle of Ballynahinch. Richard Martin, Nimble Dick's grandson, was the first of the family to be educated (at Harrow and Oxford) as a Protestant; he became Member for Galway in the Irish Parliament and, after the Act of Union in 1800, at Westminster. Nicknamed Humanity Dick by his friend the Prince Regent for his legislation on animal welfare, and known as Hairtrigger Dick for his notorious duels, when quizzed on this contradiction between his attitudes to animal and human life he replied, 'Sir, an Ox cannot hold a pistol!' Richard Martin was in all senses an extravagant figure in London society, and Ballynahinch was his necessary refuge from controversy and bailiffs. It seems that the Martins were less oppressive than several neighbouring landlords, and folklore remembers them more kindly; Richard Martin is said to have used the old O'Flaherty island-castle as a prison for peasants who mistreated their animals, but his relationship to his tenantry was more that of a patriarch than of an evicting and rackrenting absentee. The outside world, lifting its eyes from the pages of Sir Walter Scott, found the idea of the Martin kingdom immensely appealing, with its high-spirited defiance of civil law, the devotion of its wild clansmen to their master, its fabled hospitality floated no doubt on a sea of smuggled brandy, and its backdrop of trackless wastes and stormy skies. Charles Lever used Ballynahinch as the setting of a novel, while Maria Edgeworth and Thackeray were among those who visited Richard's son Thomas Martin in the days when he was called the King of Connemara and his daughter Mary its Princess.

This veil of romance was torn away by the Great Famine, revealing a death's-head landscape. Reports from Connemara were as terrible as those from anywhere in Ireland. The Martins, bankrupted by generations of high living and the general collapse of agricultural profits that followed the end of the Napoleonic Wars, could do no more for their starving people than the worst of the evicting landlords. Thomas went to visit his former tenants in the workhouse, caught the famine fever, and died; Mary inherited only debts, and fled to Belgium with her newly married husband. The estate had been mortgaged to the Law Life Insurance Society of London, who soon had it put for sale, with the vulturish commendations I have quoted above, and when there were virtually no bidders, bought it in very cheaply. To make it a saleable property they set about clearing the land by evictions, and, being as well versed in Scott as any, added battlements to the Martin's plain house. However it was not until 1872 that a London brewer, Richard Berridge, took the bulk of Connemara, plus a few small Mayo estates, off their hands for £230,000—nearly a quarter of a million acres at just under a pound an acre.

I have summarized this history in terms of a few prominent names; but who were these historically anonymous folk who, for their betters, appeared as a mere natural feature of the landscape, to be cleared like scrub when no longer a source of profit? Many of their surnames recalled days that had become glamorous in retrospect: the O'Flahertys were still numerous, and the O'Malleys who looked back to a comparable glory in west Mayo; an even more aboriginal name was that of the O'Queelys, one-time chiefs of the Conmaicne Mara. The O'Hallorans and O'Duans had been stewards to the O'Flahertys, and the O'Lees their hereditary doctors. The Joyces were originally Norman-Welsh and had settled in the north-east of the area under the protection of the O'Flahertys. But all these, together with a few families that had followed their transplanted masters into Connemara in Cromwellian times, were long reduced to a common level. They were Catholic, visited holy wells, revered saints no one outside of Connemara would have heard of. They sang, prayed, mourned and cursed in Irish, and they had their famous story-tellers and poets. They lived in clusters of little one- or two-roomed cabins, under thatch; they farmed on the ancient system known as rundale, each household having a scattering of little stone-walled plots and pastures intermingled with those of their neighbours on the improved land near the village, and the right to graze a certain number of sheep or cattle on the huge commonage areas of bog and mountainside further away. They fished from hide-covered canoes or small wooden sail-boats, cut turf from the bogs and ferried it to the Aran Islands and Galway city for sale as fuel, and gathered seaweed for kelp-burning on the shore. Since their work called for many hands, and extra plots to feed them could always be won from the margins of the limitless bogs, early marriage and lots of children were advantageous, and the population, especially in the coastal areas, grew astoundingly, until it was a puzzle to visitors what they could all be living on.

From the landlords' point of view these folk were primarily a potato-fed, rent-producing stock. The potato, most years, produced a filling if monotonous food-supply out of small patches of earth well manured with seaweed, so that every other product of the hills, the bogs, the sea and the shore could be sold to pay the rent. As a Roundstone man observed to a visitor in 1844:

Three hundred and sixty-five days a year we have the potato. The blackguard of a Raleigh who brought 'em here entailed a curse upon the labourer that has broke his heart. Because the landholder sees we can live and work hard on 'em, he grinds us down in our wages, and then despises us because we are ignorant and ragged.'*

And when the potato failed, as it did periodically because of drought or excessive wet or disease, these ragged ones starved, or

---

* Asenath Nicholson, *Ireland's Welcome to the Stranger or Excursions through Ireland in 1844 and 1845 for the Purpose of Personally Investigating the Condition of the Poor* (Dublin 1847).

emigrated; occasionally there were government road- and harbour-building schemes on which the able-bodied could earn a pittance, and scraps of charity to be begged from the upper classes.

Whereas their neighbours the D'Arcys had developed a town and a port complete with warehouses on their land at Clifden, the Martins had left their estate largely unimproved. The only settlement on it that was more than an agglomeration of cabins was at Roundstone, where the engineer Alexander Nimmo had leased land around a harbour he had built there for the Fishery Board in 1822, and then sublet plots along the new road he had laid out, and so brought into existence a neat village, which had flourished for a few years with the herring fishery, and then had fallen into decline. In general the teeming population of Connemara lived from hand to mouth, unable to lay anything aside against bad times, while most of the Martins' rent income was wasted in profligate living abroad or sunk in ill-advised mining ventures at home.

Thus when the potato blight struck in four successive seasons from 1845, there was nothing the smallholders, the landless labourers and the fisherfolk could do but plead for a job breaking stones on the Government works, and when those were shut down, sell everything they had, including spades, nets, boats, and even their clothes, to buy food, and then abandon everything to face the horrors of the emigrant ships from Galway or the fever-ridden workhouse at Clifden. Connemara's agony was of course shared by most of Ireland. Sir Robert Peel's Tory government and its civil servants reacted energetically to the emergency at first, but, given the general underdevelopment of the country and the ignorance of science as to the nature of the potato blight, their best efforts could not have averted the disaster. The shameful record of the Whigs under Lord John Russell, after the fall of Peel in 1846, cannot be expunged by historical revision; here was a ruling class of immense wealth and power letting its humanity be overruled by the idea that laws of economics were laws of Nature and therefore laws of God—always an attractive belief to those in whose favour the so-called laws are working. In 1847 the new government transfered the cost of famine relief onto the Poor Law rates. The result in Connemara was typical: since the rates were levied locally on property owners who themselves were being bankrupted by the loss of their rents, the workhouse had to close, and its desperate inmates were sent out into an utterly destitute world. By the time of the Law Life sale in 1849, another total failure of the potato crop, and the spread of typhus, relapsing fever and dysentry, had seen to it that, indeed, 'the same Tenants by name, and in number,' would not be 'found on the Lands'.

✻

Human life sheds evidences of itself in chaotic drifts; History salvages a handful of leaves from the rainstorms and bonfires of that perpetual autumn, and tries to imagine the forest. Here, in this present publication is a leaf that has preserved some sap and colour. It is a journal, the manuscript of which surfaced at an auction in England in 1994, and it covers a few weeks in the life of a young Scottish surveyor, one Thomas Colville Scott. The background sketch I have offered above will make its opening entry quite explicit:

London Thursday, Feby 3rd 1853: Left London this afternoon, by the 5 p.m. Express Train, for the County of Galway, Ireland, to execute my first important Commission, namely, to survey, value, and report on, the 'Martin Estate', Connemara, in conjunction with Mr. E.P. Squarry of Salisbury, and Mr. Hitchins, mineral Engineer, London; for a group of gentlemen represented by Mr. 'Coverdale, Solicitor, Bedford Row,' and who propose to purchase the entire Estate, containing nearly 200,000 acres, from the 'Law Life Insurance Company'.

One senses immediately the energetic, factual, commercial temper of Victorian England working like pistons in that 5 p.m. Express Train out of London. But the efficiency of the railway system, recently extended to Galway, only delivers the young surveyor all the more promptly into a land stunned by misfortune. When, five weeks later, back by his own fireside in 'the great Metropolis', Colville Scott tries to arrive at general conclusions, his mood is very different:

If, now, I take a retrospective glance at the scenes and the people I have just left, how puzzling the theme, how vague the thoughts, how indefinite the resolution!

And although he goes on to assure himself that the 'state of Ireland' cannot just be a mystery, that it must arise from known historical circumstances, his attempts to explain the horrors he has seen fall back on the colonialist presumptions of his times: the benightedness of the Roman Church, and 'Paddy's' fecklessness; and he concludes a conventional analysis with a stirring appeal to Ireland to emulate his own country, Scotland, in throwing off the trammels of a creed inimical to self-reliance and progress. This historical, political and economic summation is worth reading as an example of ideology at its largely unconscious work of justifying exploitation, and it is salutary to see the benightedness and fecklessness of capitalist thought so exposed. But much more valuable are his day-by-day notes, his unsentimental and spontaneous descriptions of the people he meets as he probes into every corner of the wreckage of the Martin estate, individuals who, whether they are traumatized to the point of imbecility, or are bettering themselves on almost invisible means, are at least spared the final ignominy usual to famine victims, that of burial in statistics.

Colville Scott comes to Ireland with a full hand of stereotypes of Irishness. At each stop of the train journey from Dublin to Galway, he sees intending emigrants taking leave of their loved ones, a sight, he remarks, that from repetition ceases to be affecting and becomes ridiculous, '... especially when you see two unshaven greybearded men, hugging and kissing each other, until as much friction is produced by the contact of their chins as would result from that of two friendly New Zealanders' noses.' This ugly distancing of the Irish to the antipodes of civility (of which the journal *Punch*'s insistant portrayal of them as simians was a more extreme version) is laid aside later on, as the enormity of Connemara's wrongs is forced upon his attention. It may be that a temporary breaking-down or at least a reorientation of his prejudices shows itself in some of the emendations he makes to his journal. For instance on the journey across Ireland he notes that people in the fields stop work to watch the train pass by, 'a matter of course with the Irish'; but this phrase is crossed out, perhaps because after having come across instances of painstaking industry in Connemara he comes to the conclusion that the problem with Irish labour is not laziness, but a want of sensible direction.

Among the minor misfortunes visited upon Connemara in the 1850s was a determined attempt to make it 'come out from Rome', headed by an English clergyman who was convinced that the Famine had been sent by God to further that end. Colville Scott is of course a church-going Protestant, and attends morning service at the Episcopalian church in Roundstone on the day after his arrival at Ballynahinch. The subject of the sermon is Transubstantiation, and it is not, he feels, handled 'in a way likely to enlighten the understanding or improve the feelings [of] the congregation consisting of those patted children who are so ardently pounced upon in the west as the fittest subjects for proselytism.' He finds that there is almost open war on foot between the Roman Catholic priests and the Protestant missioners, and notes that 'this work of conversion is done with rather too much chuckling triumph over the Roman Catholics to obtain the support of others than the interested casuists.' Indeed the evangelical exploitation of misery in post-Famine Connemara, the contamination of charitable works by the use of food as a religious persuasion, was a shocking episode, and one is relieved to see that young Colville Scott, an average sensible Briton, is repelled by it. As if in grim mockery of the theme of Transubstantiation, it is in returning from this consideration of theological niceties that he first comes across 'the rude graves in the Bogs, Quarry holes and even on the ditches, into which the unfortunate people were flung in the time of the famine of '47':

The very dogs which had lost their masters or were driven from their homes became roving denizens of this district and lived on the unburied or partially buried corpses of their late owners & others, and there was no help for it, as all were prostrate alike, the territory so extensive, and the people so secluded and unknown.

On the following days, with three inches of snow on the ground and the roads icy, he explores the north-western peninsulas, and views a part of the estate from which hundreds of poor tenants have been driven off 'by a combination of Soldiers, Revenue Officers, and the Constabulary.' There are still hordes of squatters and 'unrecognised subtenants who pay to the middleman double his entire rent'.

I saw these subtenants at work, most of them widows, forsaken wives, and young women, carrying peat on their backs. They were nearly in a state of nudity, and appeared, from actual want, to be reduced to a state of Idiocy. There is no Irish animation here, but a stealthy and timid look, as if the poor souls were ashamed of their condition, and lost to the faintest hope of escape from wretchedness and misery. Good God! where are their Landlord & the responsible power that rules over them: have they never looked into these all but vacant faces only animated with a faint imploring look—have they never seen the bent back of the aged, and the sunk cheek of the young? then let them come here and see what neglect has done.

But at the end of that bitter day he is cheered to encounter a young woman who rents a 40-acre farm, manages a dozen or so men and women, paying them no wages but cooking well for them, and sells her eggs, butter and corn in Clifden market. Such contrasts reoccur as over the following weeks he quarters the estate. There is, he finds, here and there in Connemara land that, if it were not overdivided between holdings, has productive potential, but the problem throughout most of the region is that the cultivable plots are too small to be ploughed and too scattered to be united into farms big enough to provide more than mere subsistence; in fact the only people who could live off this terrain are the spade-wielding smallholders who have created these patches of tilth. (In this conclusion Colville Scott is in agreement with recent ideas in historical geography:* the rundale system was not an obsolete antiquity preserved in the far west by isolation, but a sound adaptation to the ecology of the human habitat; only the constant drain of resources through rent, and the imposed dependence on the potato, made the society based on it so vulnerable.) However, mere sustainable subsistence is not what life is about, in Colville Scott's eyes. Throughout the region he finds that

Every spot of [soil], however limited in extent, barren in productive powers, or inaccessible in situation, is turned up, and, in many cases, beautifully tilled. I always feel a sorrowful regret to see so much mistaken industry,—the crops do not half repay it; no English laborer would undertake a tithe of the toil for the whole reward; and in fact it looks like a blindfolded war with nature, in which Paddy does himself great injustice, there being no fair field for him.

A fair field would be one that lets 'Paddy' produce a surplus for the landlord, of course, and there would still remain the problem of surplus humanity not requisite to this end. Although Colville Scott is troubled by the inhumane execution of clearances, he does think that giving the tenant a bit of money to go elsewhere is a sensible procedure. Thus when on a neighbouring estate he comes across a poor widow and her boy sitting in the snow falling into their roofless cabin, he is moved to give her a shilling and inquire into her situation; but on learning that the landowner, Lord Campbell, is allowing ejected tenants all arrears of rent and ten shillings more when the roof is pulled off their cabin, he comments that 'This proceeding, though apparently a harsh one, is wise and necessary to prevent a recurrence among these unguided people, of pestilence, famine, and untimely death.' The fact that the cabin was their home does not obtrude.

We do not have Colville Scott's final report to his London clients, but it was no doubt negative, since it was to be another two

---

* For instance, Kevin Whelan's introduction to *Letters from the Irish Highlands of Connemara, by the Blake family of Renvyle House 1823–1824* (Gibbons Publications: Clifden 1995).

decades before Capital decided that there was a fair field for its own operations in Connemara. Instead, the manuscript concludes with his painfully excogitated attempt upon 'the Irish question'. So the value of his testimony is not in its depth of understanding, but in some human images he transmits as it were before he has had time to muffle the shock of personal encounter in social theorizing. One of these, both starkly elemental and richly individuated, is likely to haunt the readers' mind as the very personification of that inhabited desolation, Connemara after the Famine:

… an Irish curiosity, namely a *Chimney sweep boy* about ten years old, and three feet high; he had run away from his employer in the town of Galway, and had reached this out-of-the-way spot, 60 miles distant, *without a stitch of clothing, except a belt of sacking, about one foot in width,* around his waist! When we met him, a thick shower of snow was falling, and he was running along with his hands over his shoulders and a little *hoe* under his arm. I stopped him and asked his history. He laughed and told me— adding that he had just swept the Priest's chimney, and was on his way to do the same good office at the Constabulary Barracks. I asked where he put his money when he got it, and he said, in his hand, 'but' said I, 'how will you do when it accumulates?' 'Oh,' he replied, 'I'll fall upon a plan when that occurs.'

Surely this apparition is William Blake's chimney-sweep, mysteriously transported from London:

> … little black thing among the snow,
> Crying 'weep, weep' in notes of woe!

—except that, in Connemara, he is laughing. Colville Scott sensibly arranges to have him scrubbed and provided with a coat; and, in his journal, brings home to us that appalling laughter.

A NOTE ON THE TEXT

The manuscript of Colville Scott's journal and concluding general essay is a leather-bound octavo volume, currently in the possession of Mr Neville Figgis of Dublin, whom we thank for giving us the opportunity of publishing it. Some remarks in the journal suggest that it was written up from memoranda made on the spot and day by day, and that it was intended for circulation among family and friends. Spaces were left for illustrations here and there, and most of them filled in with drawings based on engravings in contemporary guides to Ireland, notably those by Mr and Mrs Hall; only one or two sketches appear to be original. There are many emendations, especially in the concluding essay, where the force of Colville Scott's rhetoric nearly capsizes him. In fact it may have become clear to him, finally, that the volume was not presentable as it stood, and the work of illustrating it seems to have been abandoned.

The text has been transcribed for this publication very literally, preserving oddities of spelling and punctuation for old Time's sake. A few crossed-out passages that are still legible and of interest have been included {and are enclosed in braces, thus}. Section numbers, square brackets and parentheses in the concluding essay, evidently inserted after its completion, perhaps as part of some uncompleted editorial process, and perhaps not by Colville Scott, have been left in place. Otherwise the only changes that have been made are the replacement of double by single quotes, and the use of italics, instead of underlining, for emphasis.

Roundstone , September 1995

*This diary was written by Thomas Colville Scott
on his first visit into Ireland.*
H.D.C. SCOTT.[1]

Lynch's House, Galway Town
(Spanish architecture)

Ireland
Journal
of a visit to
Connemara
Galway

London

Thursday, Feby 3$\underline{rd}$ 1853

Left London this afternoon, by the 5 p.m. Express Train, for the County of Galway, Ireland, to execute my first important Commission, namely, to survey, value and report on, the 'Martin Estate', Connemara, in conjunction with M$\underline{r}$ E.P. Squarry of Salisbury, and M$\underline{r}$ Hitchens, mineral Engineer, London; for a company of gentleman represented by M$\underline{r}$ 'Coverdale, Solicitor, Bedford Row,' and who propose to purchase the entire Estate, containing nearly 200,000 acres, from the 'Law-Life Insurance Company'.

Reached Dublin at 6 ¼ a.m.; called at 'Andersons Hotel' for M$\underline{r}$ Squarry and left Dublin, by the 7 a.m. train of the 'Midland Great Western Railway', for Galway. There is much good land along this line, especially about 'Mullingar' and 'Athlone'.

The capacious Barracks at both these places, and throughout Ireland generally, strike *strangers* with their prominence as compared with the works of an industrial and a peaceful character, and with the poor native hovels of the inhabitants; they soon learn, however, that these are 'the national Institutions' of Ireland.

On approaching Galway, the Land,—to use an 'Irish Bull',—becomes a bed of Rocks and stones, pertaining to Granite and Limestone,—the herbage is sweet on the spots where any soil exists.

There seems to be seaweed brought in by the tides to the very head of Galway Bay, and this is used for topdressing grass, and manuring potatoes. Saw several men and women planting potatoes in these patches; all of whom,—ensconced in great coats,—immediately suspended operations when the train was passing {—a matter of course with the Irish}.

At several intermediate stations on this line, I witnessed emigrants taking their departure for America, by Dublin and Liverpool. These partings are affecting to those who witness them for the first time, but they soon become ludicrous, from their boisterous grief and wailings, especially when we see two unshaven greybearded men, hugging and kissing each other, until as much friction is produced by the contact of their chins, as would result from that of two friendly New Zealanders' noses.

Put up at the 'Railway Hotel', a gigantic building, just opened to the public.[3] In the afternoon, walked round the town, which contains some fine Squares, many good houses, with a dense, and to infer from the crowded state of the streets, an idle population.

Inspected the navigation works now in progress on the

lower end of Lough Corrib,—a splendid stream from which rushes through the centre of the town. Saw a young English Surveyor sounding and measuring the lower end of the Lough, with happy complacency, diverting himself with the ready jokes of his Irish assistants, who were *leisurely* taking soundings up to the haunches in its waters.

The connecting link now making by means of a short canal and locks between Galway and Lough Corrib will evidently facilitate internal trade; but I am at a loss to know what the new traders on the Lough are going to carry, seeing that the surrounding country is all but hopelessly barren. Summer excursions on the Lough may become common, in consequence of the facilities of transit afforded by the Railway to Galway, but this is altogether inadequate to induce the expensive improvements going on there; it also appears to me that Galway can never be made anything but a port for Ireland and not for America, as is fondly hoped by the men of Galway.

Ancient doorway in the Town [4]

Saturday Feby 5th

Left Galway, at 10 a.m., by Bianconi's car,[5] for Ballynahinch, a distance of 44 miles. In the immediate neighbourhood of Galway there are numerous clusters of Cottages of the poorest description, and whenever 10 square yards of soil can be found between the rocks, it is scraped up with exemplary industry into 'lazy beds' for potatoes. These patches, although appearing to be only a light sharp loam, incumbent on decomposing Granite and other rocks, must be of a very fertile nature, for they are invariably planted with potatoes, year after year, and continue productive, though no manure is raised and applied them. These small patches continue for ten or fifteen miles along the road, and if ever the painstaking squatters, now upon them, are superceded by larger Farm Tenants, they must all be laid down to grass, as it would be impossible to till them with the plough as they are, and it is equally impossible to clear them of stones and lay them together. Being on the margin of a limestone formation, the herbage would soon become good and sweet.

Many Farms could be thus formed between Galway and Oughterard, suitable for Dairy Farmers wishing to keep from 10 to 30 Cows; but this would involve a *present outlay* and likewise *a great sacrifice of annual rent* to the existing owners of the land. The prescribed national system of allotments seems then to have a natural origin here, and be best calculated to afford fair rent on an average of years and to sustain and supply the population. The Bogs between Oughterard and Ballynahinch are immense in extent, and apparently all drainable, and worth improving.

There are gravelly subsoils everywhere in conjunction with these Bogs, which if spread on the surface would, of itself, produce herbage of a useful description. The water from all these Bogs, is *pure*, showing the Bog soil to be of a different character, from that of the English and Scotch Bogs, exuding their black and poisonous waters.

The Limestone[6] in this district is very frequently blended with decomposing Granite, but here and there it is found pure, and burned with peat turf for Lime.

Suitable and economical buildings could be put up for new Tenants along this line of country, and the shootings and Fishings preserved and let to advantage,—at present this is all neglected, and there is stock on the lands.

Reached Ballynahinch at 4 p.m., having walked from the Oughterard and Clifden road to the 'Castle', a distance of about a mile. Met M[r] John Robertson[7] and his wife on the road. M[r] R. is a Dumbarton man and came here about twenty years ago to fish the Salmon rivers and the Oyster beds in the Bays of 'Kilkerrean', 'Burterbuy'. He has a lease of these fishings, and also of some land, and seems to have managed all his business well, both for himself and the poor people in the district whom he extensively employs. When the Martin Estate came into the hands of the 'Law Life Insurance Company', in 1848, M[r] R. was appointed their Agent, being the only person resident in the district who had sufficient knowledge of the people and energy to manage them. He has a salary of £500 a year and £100 for expenses and now resides in the 'Castle of Ballynahinch', having an office near at hand, where two Clerks are constantly in attendance to receive rents from the numerous O's on the Estate.

Two nephews attend to his interests in the fishings, namely Mʳ Wm. Robertson,—son-in-law of Mʳ James Pendlebury of the Dukes Dock, Liverpool,—who mnges the Oyster beds,—and Mʳ James Crawford, who attends to the Salmon and river fishing. Mʳ R. Senr. has built what he calls a 'Hotel' at the Salmon Weirs about a mile from the Castle and he thus avoids the expensive luxury of Irish hospitality in which 'the Martins' used so freely to indulge.

He has built some Cottages for his men, and preserving houses for the Salmon and the Oysters, which are boiled in Canisters, hermetically sealed & then sent to Dublin, London, and other markets.—

Sunday, Feby 6ᵗʰ

Drove from Ballynahinch House to Roundstone Episcopal Church, 6 miles. The Rev. Mʳ Ashe, the incumbent, read the service, and Mʳ Brook from London, preached. The subject was 'Transubstantiation', which he handled with considerable 'cunning of fence' but not in a way likely to enlighten the understandings or improve the feelings of the congregation consisting principally of those patted children who are now so ardently pounced upon in the West as the fittest subjects for proselytism. There appears to be 'open war' waging at present between the Protestant and Roman Catholic Clergy, headed by the Rev. Mʳ Dallas[8] of London, who was lately here, and is establishing Schools in almost every parish, & even in isolated spots amongst *rocks* and *lakes*, which appear almost inaccessible. These Schools are drawing in many deserted or orphaned Roman Catholic children & the converts are opprobriously designated 'Jumpers',—This work of conversion is done with rather too much chuckling triumph over the Roman Catholics to obtain the support of others than the interested casuists.

The village of Roundstone is nearly all under a principal Lease to the late Mr Nimmo,—who came from Scotland about 30 years ago, and made the principal roads in the district,—and who subleases to others.[9]

The Herring trade once flourished here; but is now gone and many of the houses are forsaken and decaying.

The land round the village is good, but the quantity available for tillage, very small. There is a monastery[10] here, which I attempted to look into, but was thwarted by the dingy screens suspended on the windows. The monks appear to have felt the pinch of the late famine & are evidently in no plight at present to join in the jolly chorus of the Friars of old.

In going and returning from Roundstone, I looked at many of the rude graves in the Bogs, Quarry holes and even on the ditches, into which the unfortunate people were flung in the time of the famine of '47. The very dogs which had lost their masters or were driven by want from their homes, became roving denizens of this district & lived on the unburied or partially buried corpses of their late owners and others, and there was no possible help for it, as all were prostrate alike, the territory so extensive, and the people so secluded and unknown. The luxuriant tufts of grass and heath shew the spots where they lie.—

Famine 'Scalp' or Hovel

Monday, Feby. 7th

Commenced surveying the Martin Estate this morning and was overtaken by a snow storm: Well provided against it, and therefore proceeded.

Drove about four miles up 'Emlachduroe' and 'Barnanorann' mountain: On the north side of the latter is a Green Marble Quarry, once worked for a short time, and the produce shipped in its rough state from 'Timbeola' Quay to London, but now suspended. Took up several small specimens. From this Quarry to the 'Owenglen' river on the north, the Relief Commissioners constructed a road, intending that it should extend to 'Ballynakill' harbour, but, like nearly all similar undertakings in Ireland, it was left *unfinished*. *Irish like*, too, they completed it as far as the banks of the 'Owenglen' river,—the width of which is about 40 feet, and the perpendicular height of the banks, six feet,—and being unable to provide funds to build a bridge across, they expended the residue of what they had in hand, in continuing the road through the Bog on the *opposite side*, for about two miles, thus bringing travellers to a point constituting an 'Irish predicament', and involving the necessity of wading up to the haunches through the Owenglen river, or of returning![11]

'Cregg', the first Townland we visited, consists of one large mountain of cold, stiff bog and clay, and about two thirds rocky and meadow pasture. Visited the only house upon it,—occupied by a Shepherd. There are a good many promiscuous cattle on this Holding, and a few sheep. The Shepherd has two or three assistants, although the same work would not be considered half employment on a Highland Farm in Scotland for one herd. The wages given to each man is though only 50/- or 60/- p.ann., and a free house, and potato ground, are nearly equal to the annual rent of the Land. The sheep are of the Connemara breed, resembling the smaller cheviots, with finer in the wool. The cheviots are evidently adapted to this country, and would be more salable.

This Lot contains two marble quarries, both of which I looked at.

'Tooraskeheen' was the next Holding visited, on which there is some good arable land, also some excellent 'marsh meadow', if managed as it would be in England.

The mountain pasture is partly poor and bare rocks and stones, the soil & herbage having apparently been blown off, and there is a small part of improveable Bog.

Lot 95, 'Loughanna', has some good *old* Arable land at the head of the Lough of the same name, now in pasture. The aspect of all the best land is Northern. The mountain top is all Bog!

The singular phenomenon of these Lots, is the sight of 140 lakes from the top of the mountain of 'Cregg'.[12] The guide who accompanied us, with genuine Irish exultation, claimed 365 lakes,—or one for each day in the year,—which he said, made it 'the finest view in the whole world entirely', but on an experienced settler in the district, who was with us, hinting that Pat would consider a stray sheep within his territory, a much *finer view*, and that he had eaten more stolen 'muttons', than the said number of days, our credulity in the marvels related by Pat was considerably diminished. We, however, counted upwards of one hundred lakes, apparently under our feet, and on which the sun was glistening with fine effect: the ocean was within eye shot in the distance, and the whole constituted a view which has no parallel.

The base of this Mountain is full of badgers holes, and badgers and foxes are reported to be numerous, and most destructive to the lambs in Spring.

These three Lots would make a very good holding for one respectable Tenant, with a capital of a £1,000, but where is the inducement for a Native Capitalist, or an industrious stranger, to disturb the present occupants, and isolate himself here? and when, again, is the advantage to a Landlord to make such a sacrifice of annual rent, and incur a present outlay for buildings, so as to tempt immigrant tenants to settle here? The natives must be cheapest because natural instruments by which the redemption of this all but lost country is to be wrought out or it must be left to the force of time & circumstances.

At present the face of this country, & of its people, look as desolate as if the whole region was about to be abandoned.

The twelve Pin Mountains & Ballynahinch Lake [13]

Tuesday, Feby. 8th

Morning, cold and Winterly, snow about three inches deep, —an uncommon occurance in the 'far West'.

Started at 7 a.m., car to Clifden, and thence to Ballynew. Here we were surrounded by a swarm of the poor squatters, about 30 in number, with their wives, sons, daughters, sisters and brothers, making about a hundred in all, who kept up a constant chatter in Irish as to the object of our visit. A spokesman amongst them put this pointedly to us, and having satisfied him so far that we had no sheriffs' warrants, we were assured, 'by dad', that it was 'all right' & the whole mass seemed to breath more freely. Hundreds of these poor tenants have been driven from this part of the property by a combination of Soldiers, Revenue Officers, and the Constabulary, and hundreds perished in the time of the famine. The residue of the Occupiers now live almost in common, except as to the cultivation and croppings of the potato patches, and thieving is understood to eke out materially their security. A

Mr Twining[14] from London, has been billeted on an adjoining Lot {by his relations, as he was not 'particularly steady', and to conciliate his new neighbours, he immediately identified himself with them,} and it is said his neighbours at first became too familiar with *his flocks* {which shewed him his mistake, & makes him now shut himself up in disgust.} & that he had some trouble in persuading them that he was not a Communist.

The state of this little Community is hopeless, and the slightest failure of the potato crop must bring absolute starvation on it if the supplies from 'Black Mail' at the same time fail.

There is a splendid view of 'Ballynakill harbour' from this spot and also a charming glimpse of 'Cleggan Bay' and its breakers.

Walked round 10 miles of the coast, inspecting nine isolated Lots in the way. One called 'Aughrusbeg', has a good house upon it, and is in a fine position for fishing and seaweed: but it is covered with unrecognized subtenants who pay to the middle man double his entire rent.

I saw these subtenants at work, most of them widows, forsaken wives; and young women, carrying peat on their backs. They were nearly in a state of nudity, and appeared from actual want, to be almost reduced to a state of Idiocy. There is no Irish animation and buoyancy here, but a stealthy and timid look, as if these poor souls were ashamed of their condition, and lost to the faintest hope of escape from wretchedness and misery. Good God! Where are their landlords & the responsible power that rules over them: have they never looked into these all but vacant faces only animated with a faint imploring look—have they never seen the bent back of the aged, and the sunk cheek of the young? then let them come here and see what neglect has done.

Inspected the east half of 'Omey' Island from the land, time not permitting us to reach it.[15]

Proceeded to 'Barnahallia' where a Dallas School is planted amongst the very rocks. There is not an entire acre of soil on fifty of surface on this and the adjoining Lot, containing 500 acres.

Finished today's work at Miss Davises, 'Logann',—a most remarkable young woman, who rents the farm, & although only 25 years of age, she manages five or six men and as many women, whom we saw employed thrashing Oats and cutting seed potatoes. She has two or three younger brothers, all of whom she seems to keep in due subjection. She sells her own Butter, Eggs and Corn in Clifden Market, and her young Cattle in the public{?} fairs. She has about 40 acres of good land along the Bay leading to 'Streamstown'. Her Servants have little or no money wages, but she said she *cooked well for them*, as she did eggs and a barley cake, for us. She is good looking, and cheerful, and was most kind and sensible, finishing her attentions to us by having a large boulder stone heated in the turf fire, and deposited in the car under our feet, the day being unusually cold, and the roads covered with ice.

Slept at M͞r Kings Hotel, Clifden, where our comfort was not a little impaired for want of hot plates for mutton chops, and a warming pan for our frozen sheets. {There was also a decided superabundance of dirt on the floors and walls, and of 'bed-fellows'.} The Landlords Status, led us to hope for better things, he being one of the Board of Guardians & Her Majesty's 'Receiver of Droits'. He has three or four young boys deep in Latin and Greek. It is becoming quite obvious, that the Irish people are giving their children classical educations on smaller means than would be thought sufficient in England, to justify parents in sending them to a mediocrity reading and writing class.

The Peat-Gatherer

Wednesday, Feby. 9th

Still frost and snow. Was surprised this morning on looking into the street, to see one person after another pass the door, with their foreheads blackened. Thought the first individual thus besmeared had just come down a chimney, but the cry being, 'still they come', enquired the meaning, and was told it was *Ash Wednesday*, and that this practice was typical of rolling in 'dust and ashes'! I could not help thinking that this was an easy, though rather dirty, way of solacing the conscience.

Drove to 'Derrygimlagh', over which I walked: saw many graves on this townland of those who perished in the famine of 1847,—hundreds died here on this Townland.—Saw a little coral sand[16] on the coast but it is too much mixed with silica or sand, as to be of much value as a manure. A poor woman was at her prayers in the Chapel as we passed, kneeling on the damp clay floor, and counting her beads.

There is no mistake about the poverty here, and it may be a key to the petty dishonesty of the natives: my colleague having dropped a new top coat from the car, in the very middle of the village, it was heard of no more, although we offered 5/- for its recovery, about ten minutes after it was missed and also called upon the village Priest to put him on the track of the thief. He was good enough to receive us friendly and treat us to oat cakes and whiskey as no coat was forthcoming, I fear excess of poverty (and) proselytizing has impaired his influence in the village.

Drove past 'Bunowen' Castle,[17] *partly* the seat of Squire Blake the chairman of the Board of Guardians and partly occupied as *an auxiliary Workhouse* and a *fever hospital,*—he having let it for these purposes. It is a shiveringly bleak spot on the seashore, surrounded by bare rocks and sand, with a remarkable cone of rock, about 100 feet high, on the west side of it, and on which is a government watch Tower. 'To what base uses may we come at last.'

The car having stuck fast in the sand between Bunowen Lake and the sea, we walked to 'Ballinaleama', the nearest point to the well known *'Slyne Lighthouses'*,[18] and the *Westernmost Land* in the British Isles. It is a bed of upwards 100 acres of pointed rocks, 40 to 50 feet above the level of the sea, interspersed with patches of potato ground and cabins. A shrewd Irish lad sat with us on this outward promontory, with a wistful eye to America, and gave us a good account of the habits of the few people who were located here. They live partly by fishing, and earn a little by going to and from the Lighthouses, about two miles distant. His father and Uncle and two of his brothers had been drowned about six months before, in returning from one of these perilous visits, and this poor lad is now managing affairs for his mother and sisters. He was a fine sprightly youth, as most of the same class here appear to be.

Wended our way to an isolated Lot, consisting of a promontory called 'Knock', reported to be a mile and a half from the spot where we made the enquiry, but found we occupied two hours in walking the distance. Now although our route was over rocks and stones and blowing sands, we estimated our rate of progression at three English miles an hour, and allowing that Pat's *mile and a half was* Irish—equal to two English miles,—the account between us would stand thus: as 2 miles : 6 :: an Irishman's veracity to the stubborn fact.

At 'Knock' we had a truly pleasing view, on the North and West was the calm ocean,—on the South two or three miles of sand hills, thrown up by wind and waves, from fifty to one hundred feet high,—and on the East was 'Mannin Bay', glistening under the setting sun, with the magnificent 'Twelve Pin' mountains frowning in the background, and almost throwing their dark shadows in the water at our feet, though fifteen miles distant.

Our Irish Guides having thus thrown us out of our calculations, we were left in darkness on this puzzeling spot, and thinking our only chance of reaching the car, almost four miles off,—was by keeping along the sea shore which is indented like the edge of a saw, or the teeth of a crocodile, it may easily be guessed how many miles we walked, 'thus worming it along',—before we arrived at our destination. We

'Clifden' & a rapid behind the Town[19]

did so, however, after an arduous struggle, to the great surprise of the carman, who could hardly believe that Englishmen were capable of overcoming difficulties which, he assured us, were considered not a trifle, even to a 'born native'!

Changing horses at Clifden amidst a crowd of the before mentioned *smutty faces*, we proceeded to Ballynahinch Castle, where we arrived at 11 p.m.

Thursday, Feby. 10th

Drove to 'Roundstone' village, from thence walked to 'Errisbeg East' and 'West' and 'Murvey', returning across 'Letterdiffe' Mountain.

On the shore of Errisbeg East and Gorteen Bay, there is a burial ground for Roman Catholics amongst the blowing sands: here and there a cross or a gravestone was peering above ground, hundreds being hid, but I was informed that in Summer, when the sands were dry, the winds blew the covering away, and exposed many of the coffins. The encroachment of the sea will sweep this hallowed spot away.

The sounds of this shore are famed for twenty miles around, for curing a lameness in cattle, called 'Cripple', from which many die if not sent here for a time when affected.[20]

There is no room for a single large Farm in this district, as the soil, tho' very good on 'Murvey', is broken into small patches amongst the rocks and Bogs, and the supply of seaweed being abundant it suits Irish squatters who can pay rent by dint of their own labor where hired labor would ruin a larger occupier.

On Errisbeg East there is the mark of an opening made some years ago for a Copper Mine, but the Ore was too poor to pay for working. Mr Hitchens, the Engineer, who subsequently visited the spot, condemned the indications as being much too weak to afford the slightest prospect of ever being worth working.

On the rocky mountain are some rare botanical plants, which I picked up, such as, *Irish Heath, Tormentilla; Gentiana; Erica limeria; Adianthum, Capillus:Veneris,* or *maiden hair;* and *Dwarf Juniper.*[21]

In addition to the view from this mountain of nearly all the lakes seen from 'Cregg', Roundstone, Bertraghboy, Cashel and Clonile Bays, lie around its base, being as good an exemplification of the origin of the name 'Connemara', or Bays of the sea,[22] as can be found in any other part of the division.—

Friday, Feby. 11th

Drove from Ballynahinch to Kilkieran Bay, to inspect the Oyster Beds or 'Banks' as they are designated here, and 'Lettercallow', being part of Lettermore Island. The distance we drove is upwards of twenty miles, yet we hardly saw a living thing on the way. At Kilkieran we hired a boat and attempted to reach the Island, but was beaten by an awful storm of wind and hail. Out of breath, in the middle of the Bay, and about two miles from any shore, we made for an Oyster Bank, about *100* square yards of which was just peering a foot or so above water, the tide being out. We ran the boat aground on it, but the wind and hail sweeping along the curling water, almost suffocated us, although enveloped in waterproofs, and formed in a shivering square for 'mutual protection'.

The storm abating, we picked up about a bushel of Oysters, and returned to land.

'Miss Catherine O'Donnell', our Landlady, now baked a loaf for us of ½ barley ½ Indian meal, the oven being a *metal pot*, set in a turf fire. We soon dispatched the said loaf, with the Oysters we had gathered and tea of our own manufacture, and then returning to our respective corners of *the* room, we sunk into the arms of

'Tired nature's sweet restorer, balmy sleep',[23]
which unlike the world

'A ready visit paid',
though fortune *didn't 'smile'*, as the Poet says, at first to secure the above consummation,

'So devoutly to be wished'[24]

Sleeping in a cottage in such a wild district, swarming with semi-amphibious, semi-barbarous Celts, with boltless door, and not even a spare chair to secure it with,—we, as a consequence, lay in a dreamy, watchful state,—and imagine our sensations, when almost simultaneously, at the dead hour of night, we felt ourselves suddenly seized hold of in various parts of the body at the same moment, without the power of resistance! For several minutes before awakening to actual consciousness, a sensation of uneasiness had crept over me, but not being undressed, and only encumbered with our plaids or mackintoshes, we imagined if not secure from molestation, we were, at all events, ready for resistance: but the stealthiness of the bloodthirsty Irish Flea had received so great a stimulus from recent privations, that we were pounced upon and made a glorious meal of before we could turn upon our enemies,—and in vain we said, or sung:—

> 'What ails these fleas they bite me so,
> I never did them wrong!'

The stipendiary Magistrate comes here periodically, and this is where he sleeps by night, and holds his court by day! It is fortunate these cannibalized companions of the Celt, do not prevent the incursions of Justice into their dominions; but I feel they will long be a barrier to fraternity with the Saxon.

'Catherine O'Donnell's' Hostlry[25]

Saturday, Feby. 12th

Started on our return to Ballynahinch, the weather still intensely cold. Found a well-to-do tenant, 'Richard Hynes', located on a useful holding called 'Carna'. He had a good stock of common sense, and improved cattle, and is the *first* thriving man we have met with on this Estate.

Visited a Roman Catholic Chapel planted on the very rocks in 'Mweenish Bay'. Climbed 'Cuillein' Hill, on the top of which is a dilapidated watch tower,[26] erected in 1800, when the dread of French invasion was rife. From this spot we had a view, in all directions, only bounded by the horizon, and as a proof of the extraordinary clearness of the atmosphere, we saw 'Kerry-head' distinctly, distant 60 to 65 miles. Until the erection of the two Slyne Lighthouses,—already mentioned, —and the appointment of a Government 'Receiver of Droits', the natives were in the habit of lighting 'Alarm fires' here at night, to decoy any ships ashore, which they had seen in the offing during the day. The unfortunate crews were generally, if not always, drowned, as the coast is ragged and rocky in the extreme, and the plunder was then divided between the native 'wreckers' and the Proprietor of Ballynahinch. It is worthy of note that all the material in the doors, floors and fine wood work of 'the Castle' was obtained in this way; but who could suppose that the Proprietor—the 'Humanity Act' M.P.— divesting himself of all modesty, would have risen in the House of Commons and claimed compensation for being de-prived of this inhuman harvest? Yet so he did, and the vestige of this 'right'—fit only to be exercised by barbarians,—is still clung to by the present owners of the Estate, (The Law Life Insurance Company) who state in their printed 'particulars of sale' that though wrecks are now less frequent, on the coast, than formerly, they are still an important source of revenew 'to the Proprietor'!

There is a 'Dallas School' planted on the edge of a beau-tiful little inlet, or cove called 'Dooeyher Bay'. I saw the infant Scholars at play,—the sea lay still around them, the bright sun sparkled in the placid waters, and all looked like the calm peace of innocence. Yet, even here, the imagination was called upon to conjure up a hundred scenes of wreck, for this was the very garner of the wrecker's harvest; and oft in midnight darkness, has many a hardy seaman struggled his last struggle with the remorseless ocean, and many a daunt-less soul has winged its heavenward flight, amidst the wild and howling elements, in this lone spot,—

> 'Leaving a vacant tenement,
> with its weather beaten hand,
> Strewn like a weed of ocean
> On the ribb'd sea sand.'[27]

'Dooeyher Bay'

Our peregrinations today terminated in a Fisherman's Cottage, on the south side of Roundstone Bay. While wait-ing for the tide to float our host's boat, we assisted his daugh-ter and a servant girl (all Connemara men whose livestock *amounts* to *two cows*, keep a servant, however numerous their own family may be) to grind some barley into meal with one of their *domestic Mills* which are simply two Granite stones, about eighteen inches diameter, and four inches thick, fixed on the top of eachother by a small iron pin: the 'Millers' sit on the floor and turn the top stone round by a small crank handle, and every minute or so, one of them puts a handful of the grain into an orifice in the centre of the top stone. These Mills do very well, where labor has no market value, and where no public Mills are, or ever can be, supported; but there are now many small *hand mills* made by English Machinists which would yield ten times the product under the same expenditure of Manual exertion. The others, however, are in universal use: and, while speaking on this point, I must remark on the many parallel cases of *misapplied labor* which prevail in Ireland; particularly in respect to the cultivation of the soil, every spot of which, however limited in extent, barren in productive power, or inaccessible in situation, is turned up, and, in many cases, beautifully tilled. I always feel a sorrowful neglect to see so much *mistaken industry*,—the crops do not half repay it; no English laborer would undertake a tithe of the toil for the whole reward; and in fact, it looks like a blindfolded war with nature, in which Paddy does himself great injustice, there being no fair field for him.

Paid six men 4/- to row us across to Roundstone—three or four miles, and from thence drove to Ballynahinch.

'Connamara domestic corn mill'[28]

Sunday, Feby. 13th

Remained at Ballynahinch to-day to muse over the incidents of the week, and view the Policy grounds attached to the Castle. There is a good field, not of land, but of rocks and water, to work upon, and the scene might be made truly a 'Highland House'; but up to the present time, the *cutting* and *carving* that has taken place, and the *unfinished* and *poverty stricken* state of everything around the Castle, has only weakened the natural romanticness of the spot.

Ballynahinch Castle & River

Monday, Feby. 14th

Drove to 'Glinsk', about *10* miles from Ballynahinch, and commenced valuing. In the course of our inspection, came upon an attempt to construct a 'Water Corn Mill' of about *half a horse power*. Thought this effort at least commendable, and complimented the Owner, who was at work; but the sub-agent, who accompanied us, smiled at my credulity and said that it was simply an excuse to dry and grind malt during the night, for illicit distillation, and that he would have it pulled down! Alas! Alas! It appears that the only attempts which Paddy makes at what seems, to a stranger, to be *settled industry*, are done from wrong motives, and thus, one redeeming point after another is rooted out of the most sanguine mind, until not a remnant of the tattered rag of hope or confidence in him is left.

Saw some hundreds of forsaken cabins on the Estate today,—*sepulchres* of those who had tenanted them while living: the fallen thatched roofs were in many cases, their only covering, in others the walls had also fallen in upon them, but all this did not hide from our view the whitened bones of many of the old and young who had huddled together, in these lone spots, to wait for death. The way in which these people formerly lived, was simply this:—they built a cluster of cabins, attached to each of which, was a patch of reclaimed Bog, or of soil scraped up amongst the mountain rocks; this was calculated on, on an average of years, to produce just as much Oats, Barley and Potatoes, as the respective occupiers and their families would require for subsistance, none ever being sold. They acquired, in a way known only to the Irish themselves, from one to three or four native cows each, or in the case of young couples only say *two sheep*, and perhaps *two goats*; these were turned out *in common* on the almost unlimited ranges of wild mountain, and waste Bog which surrounded

their dwellings, and the produce of the stock was sold annually to pay their rents, ranging from 10/- to £4, provided they
could not evade doing so, which they all felt it incumbent
upon themselves, first to attempt, either by keeping out of the
way, or pleading poverty; and in many cases they succeeded
as the aggregate amounts of what they really owed, was sometimes not worth the cost of collection. To show their power
of resistance to the payment of rent, I shall state one case
which came to my personal knowledge: having valued the
repudiator's Farm, and talked with him, face to face. His
name is 'Mathias Molloy', and he rents part of a Lot called
'Carrowndulla' at £6 a year, having 20 acres of Arable land
and a cottage, and 200 acres of mountain pasture for this
sum. Four years arrears having accumulated on this Holding,
he was summoned before the Sheriff for debt; he appeared in
Rags and pleaded poverty, but he was not sufficiently con-
vincing, and a judgement was obtained against him. Still no
cash was forthcoming, and the Agent thought it time to put
in a distress, but this was no easy matter, as the tenant's wife
and daughters, and the other female retainers of the family,
were always on the outlook for the visitors who distribute
these unwelcome documents, and they were invariably beat
off by the *gentler sex*. The Military were at last called upon to
assist the Sheriff's Officers, but the doors were all locked and
nailed, and they had no warrant to break them open. This,
however, was obtained, and another visit paid to Mᵣ Molloy,
who, when he saw resistance would no longer avail, fell down
on his knees on the floor of his cabin, and implored the
Agent to have mercy upon him, and to pity his poor wife and
'Gossoons'. This appeal being unsuccessful, he trotted off to

a neighbours and came back with £12 of *borrowed money*, begging to be forgiven the other two years' rent. 'No',—said the Agent,—*then* sighed Mr M. 'I and my little ones must die in "Oughterard Workhouse".' The Agent said they would be better able to judge of that when they had taken an account of his goods and chattels, and struck a balance. 'Oh! you heartless Saxon', said Mr Molloy, 'take the last shilling I have in the world',—putting down £18 more! '*Now* for the legal expenses' said the man of Law, at which words, 'Mathias' rushed groaning from the Cottage. His Wife pleaded with the Officers not to search the house, but they thought such a chance did not occur every day, and so they went to work. First a bank Book was found in a *plate rack*, with £54 standing at M^r M's credit. Then 12 packs of wool were pulled down from the rafters, weighing 50 stone and worth £30.—then they discovered that a good many Cows and Stirks on the mountain had 'M.M.' branded on them, and so the full rent and about £20 of expenses was extracted from all this, leaving Mr Molloy a handsome balance at his Bankers, and at home, and *ever since,*—now three years ago, he has been a *good Tenant*, and a *punctual rent payer*!

These are the 'Gentry', and the proceedings that clog the wheels of progress, and render much of the land in the Emerald Isle, *all but profitless*. For it is the character of stern integrity, and the well directed industry of a people, that makes a country rich and contented: look at the effect of native industry and simple honesty, in the naturally bleak and ungenial soil of Scotland: these characteristics constitute the secret of her success in Agriculture, her advancement in improvement, and her steady acquisition of wealth: and until they can be transplanted to other districts, neither *individual talent*, nor *industry*, nor *capital*, will insure the same results as are uniformly attendant on the exercise of these inestimable qualities in the land where they are either inherent in the people, or nurtured in their minds from the cradle to the grave. Even the Saxon tiller of the soil, while standing unrivalled for open and generous integrity of character, is wanting in a degree, in one of these elements of success, *tutored industry*,—and hence *his* labor does not leave *so large* a surplus either for *private profit*, or *national wealth*, nor does he step so lightly and buoyantly on his country's resources in times of difficulty and depression. The comparative Poor's Rates prove this; and the lagging state of English Farming generally, and the absence of conspicuous instances of the success of Scottish Farmers in England, equal to what they *work out* at home *on similar soils*, at *double rents*, shews, to my mind, that as much depends on what may be called *the inferior elements of production*,—the laboring population,—as on those who have the capital to employ, and the heads to direct them.

About 15,000 acres of land passed under our review today, being the most extensive inspection we have yet made.

There is little variety in the quality of the Lands; notwithstanding the immence area,—the greater part consisting of mountain pasture, and sound Bog: but six or seven good

'Connemara Pig'[29]

stock farms could be formed here. *Highland Cattle* is the kind of stock best suited to the localities, but in some instances, *Dairy Cows* might be kept. A good trunk road runs through the district, with a few relief branches diverging from it, and these could be cheaply continued to the sites of the buildings necessary for the new Tenants.

Tuesday, Feby. 15th

This has been an eventful day,—we have been rowed across 'Derrysillagh' and 'Cloonile Bays', by a boatman,—here called a 'Baudoor',[30]—who, we were informed, is the *only* honest man in Connemara! We have met one of Nelson's old sailors, living on a promontory of Bog, about ten yards square, projected into 'Cloonile Bay', and so secluded and inaccessible that he has been living there for years, without the sanction or cognizance of anyone. We have also seen the oldest Monastry in the West,—'Toombeola'—and examined the bones of some of the most recent Tenants within its walls. We have looked upon the grave of an entire household on a location designated 'Canower',—seven of the family being stretched lengthways in a trench, within six feet of their former dwelling, and the mother and the son, who in the short space of ten days had performed the obsequies of all those who had been near and dear to them on earth, then sank in helplessness together under the unstayed hand of Famine, even at their very fire side, where we saw their unheeded remains. When I looked upon their whitened bones peering through the rude stones amongst which they lay, I could not help thinking that I saw a woman's reproachful look, cast upon an unmindful world, while a mother's ghastly smile was shed upon those who lay around her, and who had once, to her, been more than 'the great Globe itself and all it doth inherit.'[31] Oh! What a brimful cup of misery was here,—and what a haven of happiness and peace to them had been the hope of meeting in a better world.

We have stood upon the ruins of many of the now deserted *illicit stills*, by the produce of which these people used to live,—and if the famine was more deadly to them than others—as it really was, the difference may not uncharitably be considered an infliction proportioned to their illegal and demoralizing trade, compared with honest industry.

It is a standard tradition in this part, and it is no doubt founded on fact, that the Dominican Friars,[32] who founded the Monastry and village of 'Toombeola' in 1427, and resided in it, were subsequently compelled by the Chief of the then all powerful tribe of the 'O'Flahertys',—probably about three hundred years ago,—to pull down these sanctuaries of musty Christianity; and carry the stones upon their backs,— a distance of two miles,—to build a Castle in the Lake of Ballynahinch. These ill used Monks predicted, or prophesied, that the Owners of the Estate, would,—as a punishment, see much trouble and care, and finally become extinct, and their successors whoever they might be, after them. This has been more than realized by the fate of the 'O'Flahertys', and subsequently of the 'Martins', and though one would think the curse amply fulfilled and satisfied, as no *individual* now owns the Estate; yet we returned to the Castle with a feeling akin to superstition,—for the scenes we had to-day witnessed, made us think that the very poorest of the poor were still under this dreadful anathema; and when we looked upon the ruins of the old Castle in the middle of the Lake, with the dark shadow of the mountain of 'Benlettery', resting upon, and all around it, and saw incipient decay, laying its stealthy but unmistakable hand upon the new mansion which we were about to enter, our hearts were heavy, and even sorrowful.—

The old castle in the Lake at Ballynahinch

Wednesday Feby. 16<u>th</u>
The mineral engineer having arrived last night, my colleague accompanied him on his first 'prospecting' excursion, while I attended a monthly meeting of the Poor Law Guardians of the Clifden Union,[33] to see how they conducted business. I

walked through the wards, and saw the female inmates spin-
ning, knitting, washing, and lounging; the men grinding corn
by trudging round in a horse gang,—weaving 'Frieze' &ct.;
the boys were baking bread under the *surveillance* of an experienced woman, to prevent them stealing the flour and loaves,
or passing them out of the window to sell, as I was told they
had formerly been in the habit of doing; they were also carrying water from an adjoining brook, each gang of six being
under the charge of a compeer furnished with a rod, which he
applied it their *bare feet* whenever they deviated from the rules
of working laid down to them.

Having seen all these things, I proceeded to the board
room. The Chairman, 'Squire Blake' of 'Bunhowen Castle',—
already described,—was seated in a greasy arm chair, with the
collar of his coat turned over his ears, either to keep out the
cold, which was intense, or to mellow the sound of the sweet
voices of the Guardians present. 'Mr Johns', a Papist magistrate, and his new son-in-law,—'Mr Sculley' backed by a host
of holy Romans,—Papists are fond of Hosts,—were squab-
bling for the *collectorship* of the Rates for the entire Union, in
opposition to 'Mr Robertson',—the Agent for the Ballynahinch Estate and a phalanx of Protistant zealots. The latter
proposed that his nephew, 'Mr Crawford', should be
appointed the Collector at 3ᵈ in the £. and himself accepted
as security: These rates never having before been collected at
less than 2/- in the £, this proposal struck terror into the
enemy's camp, and he carried the day. During the dissension,
the vice Chairman,—a jolly Englishman,—presented me
with a cigar, and we smoked a weed together seated in the
window!

Mr Scully, the deputy Vice Chairman,—perched on the mantelpiece, with his feet resting on the back of a brother Guardians Chair,—drew the soothing influence yielded by the said innocent narcotic, from a large Dutch pipe; while Paul Hildibrand;—a fine specimen of what we may conceive the descendants of 'Dirk Hatrick' to be, lashed the table, within an inch of the Chairman's nose, with an immense horsewhip, while advocating the Protistant side.[34]

This man is known in the district as the 'Sea wolf', and I could easily imagine the thong he wielded, sufficient to chastise a wayward walrus, or a 'wanton Whale'!

Hildibrand is certainly as fine and open a specimen of a 'rough diamond' as I ever beheld, his black curls fell in bunches on his shoulders as he shook his immense head and twinkled his small sparkling eyes at the opposing party. A homespun blue frock coat enveloped his body to the knees, a leathern belt encircled his expansive waist, and his feet and legs were encased in dreadnought sort of Fisherman's boots. He is a descendant of a faithful Dutch retainer of an ancestor of the Earl of Sligo, who accompanied William of Orange on his world glorious mission to our regenerated Land.

He now occupied 'Inisturk Island',[35] under the present Earl, and successfully pursued the conjoint trade of *farmer* and *fisherman*; and I am much mistaken if he does not possess 'sufficient *precious metal*' in the apparent dross of his composition to render him worthy of his ennobling, though subordinate antecedents. Such are the men necessary to cope successfully with insinuating Romanism, bearing all retorts with dogmatical good humour, but striking openly and fearlessly home to the truth as he sees it,—tearing the flimsy mask from slimey tongued Jesuitism. I wish there were ten thousand 'Hildibrands',—he must be seen to be admired.

In the adjoining room was a promiscuous company of clerks, collectors, surveyors and surgeons; some of them writing, some smoking, others singing, whistling, and even dancing! What would Englishmen think of a scene such as this at one of their Board meetings in a Union Workhouse? I think it would go hard for even a 'Keeley'[36] to realize its like upon the stage.

Thursday, Feby. 17th

To-day inspected about 10,000 acres of *land, and water,* around Ballynahinch. It is remarkable how short a distance the hand of industry and improvement has extended from this, the Centre of the largest single Estate in Ireland—not one mile! Beyond that line all is as nature left it. I believe if this Property had belonged to a New Zealander or an Otaheitean Chief instead of the Chief of one of the 'twelve tribes' of Galway, there would not have been *so much* of the field for man's industry tabooed from his touch; but that cultivation and improvement would have extended *far beyond* the Irish demarcation of the 'O'Flahertys' and the 'Martins'. The only real struggle with natural difficulties, that I have discovered, has been in building the old Castle in the centre of the Lake, to which I have already alluded. The difficulty of accomplishing this work would render the merit the greater, had it been undertaken for a useful or legitimate purpose; but it is currently believed that the object of its Architect was simply to obtain a more secure retreat from creditors and Law, and occasionally to dispose quietly of an enemy or a troublesome member of a rival Clan, in the 'watery dungeon'—being the Lake itself. These are the incidents which constituted the 'romantic character' of the inhabitants of Connemara in by gone times.

The Lakes around the Castle are very numerous and fine, either for boating or fishing: and the river which flows from Ballynahinch Lake under the south front of the Castle, and onwards to Roundstone and Cloonile Bays and the sea, combines many beauties of scenery along its banks, and is also considered to be the finest salmon and trout stream in the province of Connaught.

The small plantations formed by Mr Martin, add a little warmth to this spot, but a beginning can hardly be said to have yet been made to develop the beauties inherent in such an extensive field of mountains and Lakes, Rivers and Plains, interspersed with many secluded spots, and many sunny 'Banks and Braes'.[37]

Were this the seat of a Proprietor possessing 100,000 acres of the surrounding Country,—land, I cannot call it, as the area consists principally of Rocks and Stones, Mountains, Bogs and Water,—who was able to expend £50,000 on its improvement, and had, at the same time, an income independant of the rents of such Property, one of the finest principalities in the three kingdoms could be formed, not only on account of its beautiful and healthful locality, but as a political engine in the Country, and ultimately as a remunerative investment.

Friday Feby. 18th

Drove from Ballynahinch to-day to 'Maam', 14 miles. This is simply a Cottage Hotel[38] at the head of Lough Corrib. Here Cattle fairs and markets are held throughout the year, as it stands at a convenient junction of roads between 'Oughterard' and 'Cong' and 'Killerry Harbour' and 'West Port'. In the summer a few tourists reach this spot, and in winter a stray sportsman or two. We found two of the latter class snugly ensconced at the Hostelries fire side, one being 'Horace Walpole', a nephew of the late Secretary of State,[39] and the other a 'Major' something, but what, I cannot tell, unless one of the constellations called 'Ursa Major'. This supposition is only rendered doubtful by his showing himself to be more of an Opaque body, borrowing his light from the blazing turf fire which he bestrode *most complacently*, and '*viewed unmoved*' three shivering strangers shaking the snow off their dripping garments. Supposing he *might* belong to the starry firmament, and was *out of place* in the sublunary sphere, I 'blew him up' sky high, by talking *at* him with considerable vigour, and he suddenly retired to a more congenial element I presume. Mr Walpole then opened a gentlemanly chat, and asked leave to admit his dogs,—three beautiful setters,—and we at once consented that they should be allowed to take the place of his *departed friend*.

Saturday Feby. 19th

At daylight this morning we started for the mountains of Bunnaviscaun. Drove for ten miles through the Earl Leitrim's

Property: he is reported to be a good and sensible Landlord, letting his land on lease on moderate terms, and visiting his Estates annually.[40] We were now in the 'Joyces country', the family or Clan, of that name residing here; being reported, and no doubt, truly, to be the tallest and most powerful race of men in Ireland, and consequently in Europe. We alighted at the 'King of the Joyces', door, who, 'though living on a farm of the Earl of Leitrim's is also a tenant on the Martin Estate to the extent of 1,594 acres @ £100 a year.[41] We found his Majesty at home, and he most kindly pressed us to accept some boiled eggs and Whiskey. While discussing these things in the presence of Royalty, two of his 'boys' were sent for to accompany us over the Hills, and they soon appeared, they were two nice youths, 6 feet 4 inches and 6 feet 5 inches respectively. They were most intelligent and sober minded men, fairly resigned to their *fallen state*, and to the necessity of honest industry and of the *payment of Rent*.

No members of the Head of the Clan had ever before been reduced to the former extremity, but now that Whiskey Stills had been put down, and the 'Praties' had ceased to be the Poor man's friend they could no longer raise the rent by the one, nor keep hunger from the door by the other. The old King stated that nothing but 'Government Whiskey' could now be sold with safety, 'and so' said he, 'the poor man is prevented making the most of his bit of Barley, *and the Queen gets all the profit*'!

His sons informed me that a Squire Blake had introduced Scotch Shepherds and Stock on the greater part of a large Estate here, about thirty years ago, but that they had all failed and disappeared and that Mr Blake's Estate was about to be sold—in the Encumbered Estates Court.[42] If this is true, the social condition and the soil and Climate of Ireland must be peculiarly unfavourable to colonization, as the hardy Scot takes root and flourishes almost everywhere else on the face of the Globe.

The Mine we were about to inspect being situated near the summit of 'Bunnaviscaun' Mountain, a height of 1,750 feet above Mr Joyce's house, and the ascent nearly perpendicular, We had an arduous task in conveying the body of 'Mr Hitchens', the Engineer, to its destination, and only suc-ceeded in it by dint of perseverance and the aid of two haunchmen and a *stern propeller*, similar to an archimedian screw. Poor 'Hitchens'! He is sixty years of age & sixteen stone weight. He has just returned from a tour of inspection round the world, on which occasion he had visited and laid off Mines in Canada, the 'States', Peru, Turkey, and Australia, but had never had such a climb as this before. He *looked*, but could not utter, the sentiments of the poet Beattie,[43]—

'Ah! who can tell how hard it is to climb
The steep where Fame's proud Temple shines afar!
Ah! who can tell how many a soul sublime
Has waged with 'Bunnaviscaun Mountain', fruitless war'

We reached the spot at last, and while he was picking up Lead and Copper nuggets, we surveyed the numerous Bays flanking Killery Harbour, Lough's Corrib and Mask, and others of less note, all appearing at our very feet. In fact we felt as if we could almost have leapt from the spot where we stood into either of these waters. The grandeur of the view, as far as mountains and water go, cannot be surpassed.

The Geological formation, as of almost every other Mineral district in the world,—is mountainous and composed of Quartz and Primary rocks.[44]

While Mᵣ Hitchens descended with a sack load of treasure, to repose his weary limbs within the palace of King Joyce, and luxuriate upon the couch of royalty, we crossed the mountain in a stifling snow storm, and descended into the valley of 'Gowlaunlee' on the West side. The Glen is protected by mountains about 2,000 feet high on three sides, with a fine expanding opening to the south.

One of the Tenants, 'Patt Laffey' of Knockaunbaun', has no fewer than 200 goats, which we saw grazing: they did not seem to have enriched him, judging from his personal appearance, and when he told us he only got from 6/- to 8/- a head for these animals,—when two years old,—we ceased to wonder at his poverty.

Toiled back to the high road having walked about twenty miles, jumped into our Car, picked up 'Hitchens', and drove to Maam to Tea, thence to Ballynahinch Castle, where we arrived about ten O'Clock at night, almost frozen.

The horse had been stabled during the day in the Cottage of a miserably poor woman who used to live by selling, 'Potheen',—or illicit Whiskey,—but her trade had been *ruined by the Gauger*, and herself also. Her hut was only ten feet square, and she herself appeared to be in a state of bewildering poverty and starvation. She said she sometimes still got a drop at times to sell, and the excise officers would occasionally *pass* her house although aware of its possession, because they knew she must lie down and die if not allowed to sell a 'leetle' *now and then*. I gave her a shilling, which she said would keep her *for a week* to come. Her mind seemed wandering and approaching delirium from real want. These are awful sights to see unmistakably existing in a wealthy Country, but who can ever search out poverty, or even human beings, in these wild and secluded spots? Yet few would be thus neglected if the Owners of the Irish soil, and the Priests of the people, were fully awake to their great responsibilities, and would *unite* to discharge faithfully those duties *inherent in their own privileges*—which they owe to their fellow creatures and their God.—

Sunday Feby. 20th

A day of rest and peace at Ballynahinch Castle,—and in this silent and comparative wilderness, this is not less necessary than if I had all the week been a toilsome denizen of the great Metropolis,—For the immense expanse of Bog and water; the towering and commanding height of surrounding mountains, with the lone eagle soaring in the dim atmosphere that surrounds their summits: the squalid poverty that constantly meets, and almost sears ones sight at every turn, calling aloud with the voice of injured humanity for help, all tend to tire and weary the mind as much as the ceaseless turmoil of a busy world.—

Monday Feby. 21st

Drove today to the Owenglen River, the bed of which, for two miles, consists of beautiful specimens of mottled Marble. We walked along this course, breaking off specimens as we went, and brought them away as proofs of our penetration into this almost inaccessible region. We left this river to the north in order to reach the 'Pass of Gleninagh', our easiest, nay our *only* road to about 20,000 acres of the Martin Estate. This pass is *1,500* feet high, and the inclined plane to it is about six miles in length, so that it is no easy task even to reach a Connemara *'Pass'*. 'Benbeola' and other mountain tops rise about *1,000* feet in perpendicular height above this gullet, which makes the scene grand in the extreme.[45] Had I the pen of a 'ready writer', I would detail its beauties for the information of my fair friends; for sure am I that few or none of them can ever reach the spot, with the least hope of again returning to civilized society to cheer and adorn the happier home of man; but I do not own the gift, and this, too, is a scene which must be seen to be understood and admired. Not a few adventurers have had the mountain side for their bed, and the heath for their pillow, in consequence of attempts to reach this pass. The late M^r 'Tom Martin' and his daughter; Colonel Archer, his Agent, and his daughter; a Military Captain, and M^r and Mrs Robertson, the present Agent and his wife,—were once benighted near this spot. By Mr Robertsons advice, they all took to the bed of the river when it became dark, and by pursuing its course downwards they reached *a cottage within five or six miles of Ballynahinch Castle, by three o'clock in the morning,* and having sent for Clothes and conveyances, they changed and got home just in time for breakfast! Alas! for Irish honesty, *not a stitch of the clothes they had taken off were ever returned to them,* though the house in which they were left, was occupied by a *tenant* and a *laborer of Mr Martin!*

We were more fortunate and reached a Car, as previously

arranged, by *nine O'Clock*, and having made it our dressing room, we deposited our wet clothes in the boot or 'well' of the Car, as it is called, and were safely at Ballynahinch by half past ten.

A singular circumstance in connection with the Officer who accompanied M͏ͬ Martin's party is that he had just then returned from India in bad health, and was considered in a hopeless state of decline; but the result of his exertions on this occasion, and of *wading six hours in a running stream*, was a complete cure, and he is *now* living and in good health, though this exploit occurred twelve years ago.

We passed over a farm belonging to Trinity College, Dublin, in the course of the day, and could not help remarking, how much more 'well-to-do' like, the Tenants on it looked, than those on the Martin Estate.[46]

Tuesday Feby. 22ⁿᵈ

Nothing particularly worthy of observation has occurred to day, except to note the circumstance of having valued a beautiful, but peculiarly secluded place, called 'Garrowman', which was leased by the late M͏ͬ Martin to the 'Rev͏ᵈ and Dean M͏ᶜ Mahon', in conjunction with his two daughters, 'Frances Charlotte M͏ᶜ Mahon', and 'Sophia Madelina O'M͏ᶜ Mahon'; (Oh! the love of the Irish for fine names,) and by him planted and built upon, and made into a perfect retreat from the world,—is now transferred to a 'M͏ͬ Stetcher' about whom we could learn no particulars.[47] No one knows who he is, what he is, nor whence he comes: it looks indeed as if he had no antecedents, and yet he is spending about £50 a week on improving the dwelling house and farm buildings, and in employing the people in reclaiming land. Some say he is a Professor in the University College London, others, that he is a returned Convict, and between these two extreme, it is hard to come to a conclusion.—

Wednesday Feby. 23$^{\underline{rd}}$

Drove to Halfway House this afternoon to remain for the night, and meet M$^{\underline{r}}$ Hitchens who has been out in another direction. Inspected several Lots on our way, and amongst them the splendid gully of 'Glencoughan' comprising a plain of a thousand acres of Bog, in the shape of the segment of a circle, intersected by a fine stream, and surrounded on all sides but the South, with a range of mountains nearly 2,000 feet high.

Our Landlord at this *Half Way house* between Oughterard and Clifden, 'M$^{\underline{r}}$ Peter King', is a better off man than common, having a 'snug' father, a large, goodlooking and well dowered wife, formerly considered the 'Belle of Connemara', and upwards of *1,000* acres of land, for £*10* a year! Yet he has never improved a square yard of his Bog or mountain land, nor shewn the least practical gratitude for so many favorable circumstances. He also reaps great benefit from many of the Car passengers stopping at his house and taking refreshments while the horses are being changed, and from sportsmen staying here, this being the *only house* within a circuit of six or eight miles round. M$^{\underline{r}}$ King, although so backward in industry and usefulness, is, nevertheless, not ill educated or ignorant. On the contrary, he told me he had had the education of an Irish 'Ginteelman' and could *conjugate a Latin Verb'*, with any Saxon that ever came over the water! It is no doubt true that many of the poorest of the Irish are good Classic scholars, which in all probability arises from many of them being destined for Roman Catholic Priests, and others, as Laymen, desiring to be able to understand the service of their own Church.

Thursday Feby. 24th

Drove this morning at daylight from Halfway house to Kilbrickan, fifteen miles; walked to the shore, three miles, and boated across 'Camus Bay' and through a gulley into 'Greatman's Bay', and landed on 'Barraderry'. The current at the Strait leading into the latter Bay, was running at the rate of eight miles an hour as we passed through, and surpassed anything I have ever seen, some of the Whirlpools, caused by the rocks below the surface, appeared from four to five feet deep, and the rapidity with which we rushed *through* and *over them* was quite exciting, and would, I do believe, have increased the pulsation of a *'used up man'*. This current is caused by a narrowness of the passage between two large Bays, which join the open Atlantic Ocean, and ebb and flow with it.

After our day's work was over, we again reached our boat about eight miles further inland, but darkness, and a fearful storm of wind and hail overtook us in the middle of 'Camus Bay', and we were so nearly driven ashore amongst the rocks, that my fellow travellers breathed a few prayers for a safe landing, and even the boatmen all but gave in. We landed safely at last, having taken three hours to row a mile and a half, and I think it would puzzle the best navigator, to lay our course down in a Chart. One of our guides, 'Pat Maude', was struck with what is called '*Mountain famine*' on our way from the boat to his mother's house, where we were to sleep, and we had great difficulty in getting him home. He fainted two or three times, and we had to sit up with him till midnight before we could bring about animation. It appears this occurrence is not unfrequent amongst the people in these wilds: they go out, and get too far from home, and in their struggle to return, are thus overtaken and sometimes die. It arises, I infer, from a weak enervated system, and too long abstinence from food.

The Mineral Engineer, who accompanied us today, returned to the 'Halfway House', to pursue his researches along the banks of Lough Corrib, as he saw no indications of Minerals here. Not being able to spare *our* Car, we commended him to the guidance of our talkative and most intelligent landlord, 'Mr Maude' and under his auspices, thus started—

Mr Hitchens in pursuit of nuggets

Friday Feby. 25th

Inspected an Island called 'Muckanaghederanhaulia', containing 470 acres and a good stock of hares. We had a couple of Greyhounds with us, and therefore indulged ourselves in an hour's coursing. We had several splendid runs, and felt no compunctions of conscience for thus indulging ourselves, as it was the first hour we had stolen from strict business since we had commenced our work. We *seriously alarmed* several, but *didn't catch a single hare*—at which I was the better pleased.

In the course of the day; we walked over about four miles of Lakes which is a greater feat than was ever performed by an Irvingite, a Rowanite, or any other 'ite', although they have often attempted the same.[48] They should come here to practise these miracles, and if their sins sit as light as ours, upon *their* backs, there need be no fear of their sinking!

The fact is that these Lakes, which are more than 20 feet deep in most places,—are covered with a *mat of herbage*, little better than a fungus, and form that link between Bog and water, which the Zoophytes do between the animal and vegetable world.

In the morning we met an—Irish curiosity, namely a *Chimney sweep boy* about ten years old, and three feet high; he had run away from his employer in the town of Galway, and had reached this out-of-the-way spot, 60 miles distant, *without a stitch of clothes except a belt of sacking, about one foot in width*, around his waist! When we met him, a thick shower of snow was falling, and he was running along with his hands over his shoulders and a little *hoe* under his arm. I stopped him and asked his history. He laughed and told me—adding that he had just swept the Priest's chimney, and was on his way to do the same good office at the Constabulary Barracks. I asked where he put his money when he got it, and he said, in his hand, 'but' said I 'how will you do when it accumulates'. 'Oh', he replied, 'I'll fall upon a plan when that occurs.' I gave him 3d. and said if he would remain at the Barracks until I returned in the evening, I would give him a shilling to allow himself to be washed, and to get some better clothing with. This he promised to do, and I found him true to his word. To show his precocious sharpness, he said, in reply to an enquiry as to the punishment he would be subjected to for running away, when caught, 'Oh! I got to know before I started that my indenture, had *not* been signed'! I had him duly scrubbed, enveloped in an old cast off Policeman's coat, and, sent him on his way rejoicing. He was the queerest specimen of humanity I ever saw.[49]

Saturday Feby. 26th

We took leave of Mr Patt Maude and his family early this morning having paid them £1 for our cooking and lodging, for two days and two nights. This sum *for three Gentlemen*, was moderate, and so was the accommodation, as any one may judge when I state that the best bedroom *for two*, was cleaned of the residue of the Winter's store of Potatoes, and the *outer room*, of a yearling stirk,[50] a sheep, *a goat*, and a *Greyhound*, for my Colleague's use!

After a toilsome march of *18* miles across the mountain and Bog, occupying eight hours, we met our car, about six miles from Oughterard, and drove into that town.

Nothing worthy of remark occurred during the day, and we were not sorry to find ourselves in the evening, seated around 'M‍ʳˢ Murphy's' parlour fire.

Sunday—Feby. 27ᵗʰ

'Oughterard', as a town, is contemptible in every respect; the people are poor, proud, spiritless and indolent; the arrangements of the streets, irregular and unmeaning; the houses dilapidated and filthy. There is no decent cottage, nook or corner, within its area, and whether in sunshine or shower, there is a bleak and comfortless aspect over, and all around it.[51]

We found our friend, the Mineral Engineer, billeted at Mʳ O'F—'s, Post Master, Inn Keeper, Farmer, Papist, and general grumbler. The shabby genteel style in which this man and his family live, is purely Irish; and I won't be invidious enough to describe it.—I shudder as I recall the sight of the fleas dancing like grasshoppers under the table, in the centre of their best parlour. Poor Hitchens! they had made *a glorious meal of him*; he said they were the greatest cannibals he had ever encountered, although he had been in many foreign lands.

Witnessed a 'wake' over the corpse of a young blacksmith. He lay in bed in his mother's house, his face exposed, and about forty lighted candles around it. All the neighbours of a poor person bring contributions of candles on these occasions, and the family pride is as much gratified by their numbers, as an Englishman's is by the,—to me,—*appalling* and *unwelcome* display of the *purchased mockery of woe* at the funeral of a relative or a friend.

The rooms in the poor cottage were crowded day and night, from Saturday till Tuesday, and in turns the stranger women and boys, and a few of the men, took up the mournful howling, and continued the doleful chorus from the hour of death until the grave closed over the departed. This howl, at first, sounds unearthly and melancholy, but on passing a house a hundred times, during the three or four days it generally continues, as I have done, it becomes ludicrous.

As Protestantism is spreading rapidly in this district, through the instrumentality of the Revd Mr Dallas of London, these irrational and insincere practices will soon be abated and finally scouted out of this and every other town and village in Ireland.

The Episcopal Church has just been enlarged and is now a handsome edifice.

The Roman Catholic Church is a capacious one, and beautifully situated on a shelving banks of the 'Feagh'.

The Workhouse is a *palace* in appearance and a miniature town in extent; so likewise is the Barracks.—Claremount, late the seat of the Martin family, is a snug box on the stream or river Feagh. There is a Waterfall on the south, and a high wall on the other three sides erected by the celebrated 'Colonel Martin', MP to keep her Majesty's Sheriff's Officers out of his dominions, which they frequently besieged during the prorogation of Parliament. It is now occupied by a distant relation and namesake of the family.[52]

There is not another thing in this townland worthy of remark, except that there are copper mines in the immediate neighbourhood, and a black marble quarry,[53]—all *undeveloped*, of course.

The working of these Copper Mines and the Quarry had been begun, but soon left, perseverance *not* being a virtue inherent in Irishmen. They belong to George O'Flaherty Esqr, Augustus St George French MP (the latter name now dropped) Major Martin of Claremount, and the Law Life Company.

Monday Feby. 28th.

Our friend Hitchens, took his departure today, and from his similarity in expression of face to the 'Knight with the rueful countenance', I infer he has only found out 'a mare's nest' in Connemara.

We commenced near the town of Oughterard this morning, and, therefore started on foot. Passed through many spots of really good land, but all unavailable from being occupied in small patches by Irish Squatters.—Called at a 'Dallas' Boys and Girls School at 'New Village' about two or three miles from Oughterard. We found the scholars at their breakfast of '*Stirabout*',—this, it appears, is supplied from a fund raised *specially*, but voluntarily, for this express purpose, and is apart altogether from the funds raised for instruction. From this practice, the Priests designate the scholars, 'Stirabouters', 'Jumpers',[54] and other nick names; but for my part, I can see no harm in giving Irish Pauper children these physical props, for many of them come far from home and may generally be supposed to have 'fared lightly' before starting. Let the Priests supply them with Porridge as well as Pater Nosters, and then there will be rivalry in a good cause. Many of the Scholar's Parents are Roman Catholics. Each Scholar

brings *a single turf* in the morning to keep up the fire, and this
is *the only contribution* required from them. This school was
built and partially endowed, a few years ago, by a Colonel
and Mrs Lewis, and is now under Mr Dallas's, or the Irish
Church Mission Scheme.

About a mile beyond this we inspected a Lot called 'Cur-
rarevagh', on which is a good house. It had once been inhabited by one of the Martin Family; but was now occupied as
follows:—

Drawing room	—	two cows
Dining room	—	two pigs, exclusive of a man, his his Wife and three Children
Bedrooms	—	Poultry and Turkies
Staircase	—	Geese
Larder	—	Young pigs, and a goat and kid
Milk house	—	two Stirks

This is *literally true*, though some of the uninitiated may
smile,—and all this Live Stock belonged to a 'Care-Taker',
who had no right to keep a single animal.

The site of this house is as appropriate as any one could
desire,—being on a mound within a hundred yards of Lough
Corrib, looking South. The approach is natural and easy, the
land about it of fair quality, and the trees and Gardens are all
ready to adorn and accommodate a genteel residence. There
are 1,331 acres attached, 200 of which are cultivable, and well
worth £120 a year, add £50 to this for the 1,331 acres of mountain and Bog, and you have £170 a year; and if bought at my
valuation of £3,280 and £1,000 laid out upon it, the place
would become letable @ £350 a year.

All along the banks of Loch Corrib for five miles on each

side of Oughterard, there is some good soil, and many fine sites for Houses for retirement, fishing or farming.

We visited a *mine* being tested for Mr Hodgeson[55] of Dublin, by a sensible Wicklow 'Captain',—as these foremen are called, and who was very communicative. Women and men were breaking the mineral Ore brought up, into small gravel, and it was then being carted away to be shipped on Lough Corrib, for Galway, to be smelted. The 'Captain' was sorely puzzled at the fantastic and arbitrary directions this Lode took,—I hinted that he must not expect anything to go *straight forward* in Connemara, nor suppose a smiling surface would realize below what it indicated.

We passed on across a very bleak mountain, and looked down on another Dallas's School at the head of the Lough on part of Colonel Archer's Estate.[56] Saw an abandoned Mine on the same property.

On the opposite shore is a Mr Blake's house, in a fine cluster of young wood, and the spot is really enchanting. On the Lough was a large, flatbottomed boat, by which he conveyed his carriage and horses about and landed them where he wished to start from. So much for the peculiar necessities of this district.

Saw many forsaken Lots as we proceeded, but at last came to a Tenant, 'Pat Heffernon', who had actually *improved a few acres of hill land*, and was afraid his rent was about *to be raised* when he saw us. Also saw an intelligent man and a Unitarian, 'William Lyons', at whose home we finished our day's work. He had applied for a lease, *as he wished to improve*, and said he would not *move a step* until he got one! These are hopeful signs, but unfortunately they are like an Oasis in a Desert.

Tuesday, March 1st

Commenced surveying this morning on the East of Oughterard along the banks of Lough Corrib. The difference between the orthography which obtains in Ireland and in Scotland, is worthy of note, particularly in proper names such as 'Lake', the one is 'Lough' the other 'Loch'. Many similar differences occur in their respective Irish and Gaelic words, such as for a high mountain, the one is 'Pin' the other 'Ben'; for 'low', the one is 'laight', the other 'laigh', and so on.[57]

The first object of interest we passed today was a Roman Catholic burying ground—about a mile from Oughterard—bristling with grave stones of the rudest description. It was one mass of these stones,—which consisted principally of unlettered slabs, dug out of the adjacent land, and set up on end.

The usual distinctive mark of Irish Roman Catholic burying Grounds was here, namely, *a roofless Chapel*, its sharp gable ends pointing, as it were, with inanimate fingers to a better world.[58] These buildings are generally composed of rude unhewn stone, except the Chancel end, in which there is usually a narrow Gothic Window, with roughly chiselled lintels and Mullions. I have no doubt these Chapels were all unroofed either at the rebellion of 1641, or at the Revolution of 1688, and have so continued to the present hour,—a silent reproach to the descendants of the Saxon invaders. They generally stand in the centre of the Grave Yards, in many of which interments have ceased and the fences around them have been allowed to become level with the ground.

'Rushveala',—the first portion of the Estate we valued,—contains a black Marble Quarry. The stone, I think, would

Burying-ground & Ruin near Oughterard

admit of a very fine polish, and be a hundred P. Cent more valuable for mantlepiece slabs and jambs than the *Welsh Slate* which is now used to an immense extent for that purpose. At present the Quarry is full of water and the blocks that have been cut out are lying *complacently* amongst the rubbish at its edge.

Passed over one of those natural bridges,—on a lot called 'Leightgannon',—which are peculiar to these districts bordering on Lough Corrib. They are formed by the water finding its way beneath the shelving Limestone and Mica Slate,[59] and thence pursuing its cavernous course until it meets with an impediment to its subterraneous progress, when it again appears above ground and pursues the 'even tenor of its way' to its final destination in the inland sea of 'Lough Corrib'. The connecting link between Lough Mask and Lough Corrib, after passing under ground for a distance of two miles, boils up on the surface and expands into a river as broad as the Thames at Richmond.

A Lot called 'Porridgetown' would indicate that some

Migratory Scot had been there before me, but as no other trace of 'Sandy' but the name is left, I infer he had not been able to extract either 'brose' or 'bannocks O' barley meal' out of so ungrateful a spot.[60] The poor Irish, however, were busy scraping the little soil there was amongst the rocks, into potato beds, and I must again express my regret to see so much *misapplied labor* and all for want of a knowledge by these willing people that the world is full of more legitimate fields for their exertions.

The waters of Lough Corrib wash the very doorsteps of a good many of these people's houses, and there is a fine outlet for Trout fishing: but the Tenants are all restricted from putting a line in the water. They, however, avail themselves of the Lake as a high road to the town of Galway, sending down the little produce they have to spare by boat and bringing back Sea-weed from Galway Bay by the same conveyance.

An adjoining Lot called 'Shrue' is one of the sweetest spots for a country Box that I have met with. It is on the banks of the Lake into which a small peninsula projects, forming two creeks on the East and West,—and on the North is an Island and a boundless expanse of water. The surface is rather too thickly sprinkled with rocks, but the herbage amongst them is sweet—the soil is dry and healthy and the roads good. The area is 340 acres, one hundred of which are cultivable.—There is a small Orchard, some straggling trees, and a good deal of hazel underwood.

A house could be erected, and other improvements made, at an outlay of £1,000, and then the place would be well worth £170 to £200 a year for a retired residence or for farming purposes.

An adjoining area of 840 acres, called 'Kylemore', and held under Lease by a member of the 'Martin' family @ £92. a year, is one of the most peculiar spots to be found in the British dominions, three fourths of it consisting of water washed rocks, lying nearly horizontally, in detached blocks about 50 cubic feet in size. Their bed is from 10 to 20 feet above the level of the Lough, and they all appear to have been formed by the influence of the retiring tide at some anterior period, and must, therefore, be set down as of tidal formation, and being floatal had moved onwards with the retiring waters, as the substrata on which they rest is geologically disconnected with the era of their formation, and altogether foreign to their composition.[61]

We had the pleasure of witnessing a combination of five 'Irish Farmers', whose rack rent is £1.16.11 each, in the act of burning a Kiln of Lime to be applied to their lands. Their fuel was turf, and their isolated industry is worth recording.

We next inspected 'Carrowndulla', on which Mr 'Matthias Molloy',—*the rent resisting gentleman*—resides. I remarked to him that it was a sin to see a good mountain run of *1,182* acres which adjoined his lands, *unlet and unoccupied*, and that if *I* were the Owner, I would stock it myself. His reply was that I *might* put Cattle there and see them safe when the sun went down, but he would not give 'a whistle' for my chance of seeing them in the morning! An experienced companion answered me that this was the true state of the case, and no vapid intimidation and that this was the *Modus Operandi* of working the 'internal *machine*' in Ireland.

Wednesday March 2nd

Having paid our bill last night, including a breakfast for the *next morning* as it were, *we 'fared but lightly'*, and took our departure from Oughterard with *physical* and *mental* buoyancy.

Let any one who aspires to a personal knowledge of the real state of life in the Island of Saints accompany us along the road for four or five miles to the North West of Oughterard, climb some rocky steeps about 600 feet high, and descend into the unexplored regions of undulating Bog, Cragg, and water, called 'Finnaun', and here he will find it in all its purity. This district,—chiefly composed of an ocean of Bog,—extends from where we now stand to the North banks of Galway Bay,—a distance of ten miles, comprising an area of upwards of 20,000 acres, and it may well be designated the heart of the Eastern division of 'the wilds of Connemara'.

One portion of 7,555 acres has only *one cabin* for the herd upon it. Here we boiled our coffee and the eggs which were supplied by our kind hostess, who couldn't speak a word of English. While timing the latter part of the cooking operations, with *watch* in hand, I was attracted to the wonder, almost amounting to fear, depicted in the countenances of half a dozen 'Gossoons' *or* urchins, who were huddled around the fire. An intelligent Grandmother fortunately was present, and explained to me that neither her daughter nor her grandchildren *had ever seen a watch before!* It is said that Prophets have no honor in their *own* country, and I could therefore the more readily infer that these simple people had no credit in theirs, and consequently knew little about 'tick'. When I wrote the memoranda you are now reading in my note book, they appeared equally at a loss to comprehend the meaning of the act. I gave each of the children 1ᵈ, and the Mother a shilling, and I am satisfied that neither of the former, though about *10* years old and upwards, had the least idea of the nature of money.

There had not been an animal on this Lot for three years, except the Herd's *Cow and Calf*, and a goat or two.

Yet I would not despair of making it well worth £700 a year in four years, by an outlay of £2,500 as purchase money, and £2,500 more in improvements. But who is to expatriate himself here for any mercenary consideration? Better far become a Yankee citizen in the Back woods, and have no 'existing interests' to displace or offend. The people who are squatted on these places possess benefits from such a system of occupation, and though not granted to him by the Owners, they could not be displaced with either entire satisfaction—or safety.

We trudged over all this dismal district, and after a walk of twenty miles, reached Moycullen village. In the immediate vicinity, we saw a poor widow and her boy sitting in a roofless cabin belonging to Lord Campbell;[62] and as the shades of evening were closing around us. I felt surprised at the circumstance, particularly as the ground was covered with snow. Stepping across an intervening rivulet, I enquired the particulars of the case. The answers were by no means straight forward, and I allowed myself to think that the poor body was an impostor trying to excite sympathy Seeing she could not remain there all night, as she must inevitably perish by morning, I left her and went direct to the Constabulary Barracks where I stated the case, desiring the officers to see into it immediately. One of the men said he believed she was only waiting beside her chest—her only furniture—until a 'lorry', or small cart, came to take it to the house of a neighbour who was to afford her and the boy shelter for the night. He added that she was very honest, and had lately brought Lord Sligo's great coat to their Office, having found it on the road, for which his Lordship rewarded her with a sovereign. I gave him a shilling to make it a guinea, and then felt a little lighter hearted than when I had left the hapless creature in her ruined home. I afterwards learned that Lord Campbell was clearing the whole of his wretched land of Squatters, doing this in as humane a manner as the nature of the measure admitted of, and allowing each ejected Tenant all arrears of Rent and 10/- when the roof was pulled off their Cottages. This proceeding, although apparently a harsh one, is wise and necessary to present a recurrence amongst these unguided people, of pestilence, famine, and untimely death.

From this spot the mail car carried us safe to Galway, a distance of eight miles, and we were soon seated in the splendid dining room of the Railway Hotel, surrounded by commercial travellers, Tourists and 'Tars' of Her Majesty's Revenue Cruisers, all merry and gay, contrasting almost mournfully with the scenes we had just left.

Thursday, March 3rd

Having still about 1,000 acres of the Martin Estate to inspect and value, situated in what is called the 'County of the Town of Galway', an old distinctive designation of a Barony, radiating for a distance of four or five miles around the good city of the 'twelve tribes',[63] we became 'peep o' day Boys'[64] for once, and were at work at the extreme boundary of the said division by sunrise.

'Awbwee', the first Lot subjected to our practical acumen, possessed no feature worthy of note: there was, indeed, three ruined houses and a roofless Cottage upon it, but no animated nature with which we might hold converse.

'Pollnaclogha' is just the reverse of this, namely *a live hive of wretched humanity*:—thus does Paddy exemplify as great a love for *antithesis* in practice as ever 'Dr Johnson' did in prose: on the one hand, *over population*,—on the other a *'deserted village'*. I remarked to one of the Squatters, standing at his cabin door, how charmed I was with the view of Lough Corrib, its undulating waters spread out for ten miles before us, and sparkling in the setting sun; but so far from having any feelings on the subject in unison with mine, he assured me that if I became 'one of themselves' I would soon learn to look upon the black Bog behind me,—which was 'a darling entirely',—with much more admiration than the 'sup O'Wather,'—adding that he and his neighbours cut as much Turf annually from the said Bog, for the Towns-folks of Galway, as enabled them to pay their 'rint', and 'had it not been for the blessed self O't', said he, 'we wouldn't have been able to look our landlords in the face 'sin' the praties have pleased to forsake us.'

'Tonabrocky', the next place we visited, takes its name from the fact of it being formerly a retreat for Badgers, the shingly rocks and stones with which the ground is covered, being a safe retreat for them. The similarity between the Low-land Scotch, and the Erse language of the Irish,—which I have before noticed,—again occurs in this name, for the above word, 'Tonabrocky' was interpreted to me as the 'Town of a Brock', or Badger ('Ton', by the way, is the Norman word for 'Town') and 'Brock' is the name by which the Badger is still known in Scotland.[65]

A hive of poor and unmanageable Squatters is located here, and being the spot from which the old and powerful Galway tribe of 'Burke'[66] is said to have sprung, the dread of *that name* has, until very recently, scared even the majesty of the law, as represented by writs and Sheriffs Officers from the community.

The red coats had, however, been brought into the field about twelve months ago, and by their Aid, the 'Law Life Company' had been enabled to serve *notices* on above 200 of these rustics, but they still remain, and pleaded to me that they couldn't read *'the bits O'paper'* with which they 'were favoured', and, therefore, took no notice of them!

'Bushy Park',—a unique seat of one of the Martin family[67] —possesses all the natural beauties that man could desire or money purchase. It is within half a mile of the Banks of Lough Corrib, and catches beautiful glimpses of its waters through glades formed by the Trees that embower it. Yet, for some reason or other, the house is forsaken and now falling into an untenantable state.

Below this is 'Dangan', an occupation of a hundred acres granted, on easy terms, to 'Abraham Marshall', to conciliate him after an attempt to shoot 'Bartley McAuley', one of the Martin *'Drivers'*,[68]—while serving a notice to pay rent upon Marshall's father! As a further inducement to future good conduct, he was appointed, and continues to be, *Governor of Galway Jail!* He is evidently a good farmer,—in fact the very best I have yet met with.

On the other side of Bushy Park is an embodiment of a very different social anomaly, namely 'Thomas Skilling'[69] of 'Corribview'. Mr S. is the 'Mechi' of Irish Agriculture: he has written and spoken, taught and practised in the cause; has been indicted as an enemy to *the established order of things*; a *disturber* of the 'stately step and slow' of Agricultural progression, and finally rewarded, and shelved, by being inducted 'Professor of Agriculture' in Queen's College, Galway, where there are no students,[70] and in a district so stoney that it may be said to possess no land! I recollect visiting him about ten years ago, at 'Glasnevin', near Dublin, where he was then practising experimental farming, and teaching an industrial school in connection with it. Being the son of a Manufacturer from the North, he was looked disdainfully on by the lights of the Royal Agricultural Improvement Society, and being a Presbyterian to boot, he got the cold shoulder of Priestly influence. He still indulges his taste for the science of Agriculture, and in his establishment every living animal,—and he has many,—is *pure in its breed* and a *model* of its kind. I saw 'Connemara ponies', *Cattle, sheep*, and *Goats; Peafowls, Turkey's and poultry of all kinds, Swans, Geese, Ducks* and *other aquatic Birds; Dogs, cats*, and *Canaries*; and many other native and imported animals,—all pictures. I regret that these curiosities are destined to be seen by few, the selected spot rendering it unlikely that they will be often subjected to a strangers gaze.

An immense Flax Barn stands on a Mr John Harrisons holding near this, gaping, as it were, for the crop that has not yet been sown! Paddy does things sometimes by anticipation it would appear, and we may, goodnaturedly, attribute it to their *proverbial forethought!*

Having passed over the seat and lands occupied by M^r O'Grady, the Clerk to the Galway Union, and noted the snug, orderly and comfortable like example they exhibited to the dense mass of paupers by which he is surrounded, I could not help thinking on the comforts to others that issue *even out of poverty*; yet its enjoyment must surely be subdued, if not impaired, by the consideration that we are living upon the very distresses of our fellow creatures.

With light hearts we passed through the ranks of a host of poor Tenants who awaited us on the verge of the Martin Estate, and walked into the Town of Galway, a distance of two miles, having thus completed the survey and valuation of an Estate of 191,930 acres, in twenty two working days.—

Friday March 4th

Today we looked at a house in Galway belonging to the Martin Property, and then inspected the *Court houses, Jails, Barracks, Workhouse, Queen's College*, and other public buildings, and the Town generally. It has the elements of prosperity within it to a moderate extent, but must not be supposed capable of again setting up and maintaining the useless Irish Gentry of former days, who are certainly at the present time, *not* 'the men for Galway'.[71]

Saturday March 5th

Returned to Ballynahinch Castle to put a few interrogations to Mr Robertson, the Agent, and take a final leave of him and his kind wife, and the great principality over which he rules.

On the way I was accompanied by a 'M͏ͬ Latrobe', a young Missionary under the 'Dallas scheme', destined for 'Ballynakill'. He was seated beside M͏ͬͨ Jones, the wife of a well known Papist Magistrate at Clifden.[72] This Lady's bland insinuations, and the promise of an introduction to two fine Irish girls still nestling under her maternal wing, had nearly shaken this confiding, because inexperienced, 'Knight Templar' from the elevated mental pinnacle on which he was about to enter the Popish Preserves, and open his crusade against enforced Scriptural ignorance and Priestcraft. I gave him the *cue* as to practical 'Jesuitism' in Connemara, and he shook me warmly by the hand as a proof of his gratitude, and said he would be more wary in future.

Sunday, March 6ᵗʰ

I bade adiew to Ballynahinch, leaving a blessing behind for all its people,—for the isolation by which they are surrounded, removing them, as it were, from the mellowing and improving touch of the mental and material social progress of the age, compelling them to grope their way unaided, and often misdirected, in comparative darkness, their uniform civility and willingness to oblige:—their warm, though humble, hospitality, unchilled by the bleak and stern country and scenes by which they are surrounded:—their cheerful and buoyant spirits, sparkling even in the wan eye of poverty, and pressing out from under their very rags, cannot fail to excite towards them in every ones heart, as it has in mine, a warm feeling of sympathy, of gratitude, and love.

Thirty six hours travelling by Dublin, Kingston, and

Holyhead, brought me safe to the great Metropolis, and by six O'Clock, on Tuesday Morning the *8th* March, I was once more seated at my own fire side.——

GENERAL

If, now, I take a retrospective glance at the scenes and the people I have just left, how puzzling the theme, how vague the thoughts,—how indefinite the resolution!

> 'Let observation with extensive view,
> Survey mankind from China to Peru',[73]

and no parallel to them shall be found; and this perchance may be the reason why so many transitory observers call the state of Ireland—*a mystery*. But in social questions, such as this, there can be no mystery. The various conditions of different peoples, must arise from *certain* causes, and patient and impartial enquiries into antecedent events [and Politicians] have, no doubt, long ere this found out what these are in the case of Irishmen.

The events in a Country's annals *may* be differently interpreted; but if well ascertained Historical facts are stated, the only difference that can then arise in observers' minds, is simply that of opinion as to the influence they have exercised upon a nation. While convictions then are fresh upon my mind, and facts—grown rusty from disuse—are recalled from their lethargic slumber in my memory by {a} many recent visit,—after ten years absence,—to the land that gave them birth (; and with new facts, gathered from that not uneventful period of time, added to the store,) I shall endeavour to state the views then formed, and that again arise, invig-

70

orated and confirmed, relative to this hard-to-be-understood Country and its people.

[I.] It is well ascertained, that Ireland was the earliest inhabited portion of the United Kingdom. Christianity was introduced there as early as A.D. 432 by 'Palladius', a Missionary from Milan. (The Roman Catholics claim this honor for St Patrick.) For upwards of 500 years from this period, Ireland seems to have gone on uninterruptedly in material and mental progress. The Castles, Towers, Harbours, and Forts, as also the *remains* of beautiful structures (erected and) dedicated to (higher) purposes, are ample evidences of this early prosperity. Not only were the high mental attainments of the native Irish acknowledged on the continent of Europe during this period, but even England showed her appreciation of their learning by sending her own Alfred the great to be educated at the College of Mayo,—then under the direction of the profound 'Johannus Scotus', who soon after,—in the year A.D. 800,—came over and founded Oxford College, and subsequently that of Notre Dame in Paris.

[II.] Up to the year 1,152, there appears to have been *no interruption* to *internal peace* and *progress* in Ireland. In that year, Rome issued a Bull, creating four Archbishops on behoof of its 'faithful subjects in Ireland'; but this remained a dead letter for 20 years, or until 1,172, when Henry II, to gratify his insatiable lust for conquest, invaded the country, and, aided by Pope Adrian the IV, *established the Roman Catholic Church*. Ireland thus becoming an integral part of the British empire, the native kings and Princes were necessarily dethroned and partially subjected to English rule,—and thus ended the *Milesian*[74] *Government in Erin*, supposed to have existed for 2,437 years, and to have produced 169 Kings. *Then*, in that land, began the war of antagonistic churches (and Priestcraft),—*then* Ireland became a truant from the world's great seminary—*then* did she not only cease to learn, and lie like an inanimate leviathan on the onward tide of time,—but her great heart saddened, and her mind dimmed and she gradually receded from the foremost rank in which she stood and became a willing laggard behind nations that had been her pupils!

During the wildly chivalrous reign of Richard Coeur de Lion, Ireland was not likely to fall back into the current of settled progress and improvement, and we consequently find her people in a state of continuous discord and turmoil while that King was engaged in adventurous exploits in Britain and on the Continent of Europe.—

The tendencies of his successor, John, the son of Henry the second, were of a more peaceful and conciliatory nature, but these qualities appear to have been either distasteful to the Pope of that day, Adrian the IV, or to have afforded him a better opportunity than existed in Richard's time to increase his temporal power, and so we find him issuing a Bull to interdict John from exercising the functions of a king, making him the Pope's vassal, and his entire kingdom *an appendix to the Holy See!* This arrogant assumption of the Romish Church was naturally inoffensive to now Popish Ireland, and its passive permittance by John was most probably the cause of her native Princes offering voluntary allegiance to him in 1210; but it was not until 1,216 that '*the people*' themselves showed any love for the connection with England and then only in consequence of Henry III giving them that guarantee for civil liberty, 'Magna Carta', which had been wrung from his father the year before by the nobles of England, then the natural guardians of the Saxon people. Trial by jury and other boons which the native Irish could to some extent *even then* comprehend and appreciate, were, at the same time, transferred to Ireland.

Unlike the English Barons, the Irish Nobles shewed no gratitude for these great charters of liberty, and they became, and continued for two hundred years, turbulent and troublesome, while *the mass of the people* were comparatively peaceable and contented. many of the old Irish gentry went abroad during this period, and it is well known that up to the beginning of the fifteenth century they were numerous, influential, and highly esteemed at foreign courts,—for they were always gay, and still polite and accomplished.

Ireland had little imperial guidance from the time of Henry III to 1399, when Richard II went over to revenge the death of his cousin, the Earl of March, a visit out of which may be said to have originated the war of the Roses, as Henry, son of John of Gaunt, Duke of Lancaster, availed himself of the opportunity afforded by Richard's absence from England, to come over from France and organise a force to avail him to recover his father's Estate, and his own natural inheritance, & which finally became sufficiently powerful to change the dynasty of the Kingdom.

Passing on to the reign of our Henry VIII (with his six wives) we find that he was looked favorably on by Pope Paul, and rewarded with the special title of 'Defender of the Faith', for writing a book against Luther; but on subsequently accepting from the Clergy the office of *temporal head of the Church*, and executing Sir Thos. More for refusing to own his supremacy, he was excommunicated by the same Pope,—

Elizabeth shared the same transitory favour from the Pope as her father had done, but only so long as she was a persecuting sovereign and a doubtful Protistant. When she became an open-supporter of the new faith, she was excommunicated and anathematized by the Holy See; and it is not improbable that these indignities offered to an imperious Queen, aggravated those cruel—persecutions of Roman Catholics in Ireland, which all must regret, and none can defend. The stringent government of Elizabeth, however, and the establishment of that famed seat of learning, 'Trinity College', Dublin, tended greatly to restore order, and dispel the ignorance into which the Irish had lapsed during the previous 150 years of internal feuds and misgovernment.

If we pass over the anomalous era of James VI, we come to the wretched government of his son Charles I, which combined with the still more unscrupulous conduct and tyranny of his Lord Lieutenant, 'Strafford', bore its natural fruits in Ireland as elsewhere, and in the year 1641, the politico-religious Rebellion occurred and continued for ten months during which time according to Sir William Temple, 100,000 or as ascertained by Sir Wm Petty who made subsequent enquiries, 30,000 unoffending Protestants were massacred.[75]

The 'Scrutiny of Titles' Act,—through the operation of which so many Estates of Roman Catholics were confiscated,—and the impolitic law allowing legal judges to be Privy councillors, added to the festering sore relative to *the Roman Catholic Priesthood*—who had been expelled the Kingdom in the previous reign for refusing to take the Oath of Supremacy—were the main causes of this revolt. *The territorial*

Proprietors of the soil were the prime movers in this revolt, and are responsible for the great calamities that resulted from it.

The iron rule of Cromwell was soon after this extended to redress these cruelties and crimes, and if we own the necessity of his mission, we may find a ready palliation for the ruthless hand with which he executed it—in the alliance which the Irish had formed with Rome & which was inimical to his politics & religion.

The moral and physical regeneration which begun in England and Ireland, during Cromwell's nine years' Protectorate, ought even to be remembered with pride [in] the Kingdoms over which he held the manly sceptre, And if we take hope at a people rising thus, from prostration to influence & respect by efforts of their own when guided by a Guardian hand, who will not pause in humility before *another reign* to view the Godlike aspirations of a Nation's heart, *blighted, blotted out* 'at one fell swoop', in Charles the second's reign—his people looking complacently on, and voluntarily descending with him to an unparalleled abyss of degradation.

When James II began his short and inglorious career as a King in 1685, the Irish were under the ban called down upon themselves by the revolt of 1641, and while many minds,—perhaps more generous than prudent,—were *then* willing to think that they had *fully* expiated their crime, yet none were prepared to see the Sovereign of England raise the Irish people above the amenities of subjects, and *covertly* install their Priests and Nobles in the highest offices of state. The latent Stoicism, inherent in the Saxon character, was roused, and nothing but the *most ample* retribution could allay it. The leaders of the time interpreted the nation's mind, and 'William of Orange' landed in 1688 to be its exponent. James flew to Ireland—disaffected Ireland—while William intrenched himself in England and in the hearts of Englishmen. In the meantime he sent over some of his sturdy Generals to protect Irish protestants against their own king and (their) countrymen, and on April 20th 1689 began the ever to be remembered and honoured *104* day's defence of Derry against James and his troops, aided only by his granted terms of capitulation equivalent to the fruits of victory. William, with the wisdom of a statesman, having set his house in order in England, departed for Ireland, with that *quiet determination* which marked the greatness of his purpose.

On the 14th June 1690 he landed at Carrickfergus, and on the first of July following was fought the *battle of the Boyne*. This decisive victory cost William the life of his master spirit 'Schomberg', but it ridded the kingdom of a King who was actively mischievous to half Europe and it especially restored to Ireland her famed seats of learning which had been converted into Barracks,—her peasantry which had been drilled into rebel soldiers (and her individual freedom in thought and action which had been wrenched from her by an Alien and intolerant Priesthood). James having fled to France, William soon after returned to England, leaving his able General, De Ginkle, to fight a few minor battles, and reduce Limerick, which still held out under the brave Sarsfield, Earl of Lucan, which being accomplished on 13th. October 1691, Ireland had then many concessions made to her, and improved, though slowly, in her domestic condition during the next 70 years of comparative quietude.

In the long reign of George III, Ireland had some unsettled moments, especially about the time of his accession to

The 'Boyne Water' & the spot where Schomberg fell

the Throne in 1760. It was in consequence of these indications of internal disquietude, that the Irish volunteers of 1778 sprang up, and gave their unbought services to the Crown; and if ever a type of true and timely loyalty is to be sought, we must point to that noble band, to their services, their sacrifices, and bravery.

In the year 1792, George III restored to Roman Catholics many civil rights they had, for a time, been deprived of, and thus removed their pleas for disaffection.

Nevertheless, the year 1798 saw another rebellion, which was only put down after much bloodshed, and inflicting a heavy tax upon an already impoverished country: the Royalist's compensations for losses alone amounting to £1,023,337. —The inevitable result of this last national outbreak was a confirmation of a growing belief that Ireland had become incapable of self government (and a proof of the incapacity of Irishmen to execute, with success, the limited power of internal Government entrusted to them in their houses of legislation) and the solution of the difficulty resulted (in the abrogation of these assemblies and) in the Union of 1800. This Union, while admitted as desirable in itself, is well known to have been consummated by Lord Castlereagh,— then Secretary for Ireland, under the Lord Lieutenancy of his Uncle, the Marquis of Camden,—by more zeal than scrupulous regard to niceties in the mode of its accomplishment. Be this as it may, the Act had become inevitable, and Ireland was now placed under the control of her natural Protectress, England. The embers of nationality, however, may be said never to have gone out until the death of Daniel O'Connell, which took place at Genoa on May 15th. 1847. His agitation for the repeal of the Union, and the Agitation of others for similar purposes, were the indications of this feeling, but many concomitant circumstances conspired to weaken it,—such as the visit of George IV to Ireland in 1821, the establishment of National Schools in 1828, the Catholic Emancipation Act of 1829, the Reform Bill of 1832, and the subjection of the immense revenues of the Irish State Church to the control and distribution of a *lay* commission.

(The Roman Catholic Church, however, still continued unaltered. In Ireland, she was uniting with Episcopacy to put down dissent;—at Rome, she still refused to let a Protestant worship God within her City, and those who have read the Christian and enlightened, but fruitless appeals made by the estimable Chevalier Bunsen, when Ambassador at Rome, for this privilege and the history of the Lutheran Chapel he subsequently built upon an isolated rock outside the walls, must own her want of reciprocity.)

Yet, for a little longer, Ireland continued to send forth her transported Patriots in support of what they conceived the Catholic rights, and up to the time when 'Smith O'Brien' became expatriated in 1848, even *Protestants* had not ceased to suffer in the cause.

[III.] England has given Ireland many tangible proofs of her desire for her welfare. National schools enable her *common children*, by free education, to destroy the only difference that exists between them and the wealthiest scions of nobility,—not possessed of either England or Scotland. She has (well) endowed 'Maynooth College',—another institution having no parallel in either Country. She has tendered to her, all but free secular education of a high class, by the lately established Queen's Colleges.—

Ireland is all but exempted from taxes and tolls, from Import duties and Inland Revenue. Government had provided for her poor, built her Workhouses, Barracks, and Jails: it has constructed her harbours and deepened her rivers, while the private enterprise of *strangers*, like Sir James Anderson and the Nimmo's, has constructed her roads, and the same extraneous course, through its Bianconis, has supplied the means of using them.

If we now ask what the Irish have done for themselves where shall we find an answer? In the North, where agricultural & manufacturing industry has swept want & poverty from the land, the people are immigrants and aliens, and bear a striking contrast to the pauperizing indolence & poverty of the natives in the South. In 1780, Arthur Young[76] said,—'The soil of Ireland is the richest I ever saw.'

Wakefield,[77]—'The land is of excellent quality.'

McCulloch[78] says,—'The Pastures are luxuriant and the

crops heavy.' And yet this grateful soil bears a nation of paupers! There is no such thing as an 'Irish yeoman'. The people who dig and sow are mere rent-paying machines, in whom Landlords can have little pride or pleasure, and who, in frequent vain attempts to elevate them, have been drawn into the vortex of poverty and ruin.

Since Arthur Young's tour in 1780, Rents from competition have tripled, and beggary has kept pace with their increase, & little improvement had been affected in the soil of Ireland until within the last few years.

The *ruinous effects* of the *excessive cultivation* of that best of all esculants, *the Potato*, introduced by 'Joseph Hawkins' from 'Santa Fe', New Spain in 1565,—may here be addressed, by a comparison between four of the lightest rated Poor Law Unions in Ireland, and four of the heaviest burdened with the Poor's Rates. In 1850—for every 100 acres of grain cultivated, there were:—

	People	Acres
In the four *best* Unions —— 114		14
In the four *worst* ——1,346		110
Excess	1,232	96

The internal resources of Ireland, still uncultivated, are their mines, & all but American water power, their Bogs & Wastes, their Coast fishings & game.

The time may & I hope will come when the Irish shall develop every source of wealth within their own Country, and be no longer dependant on Agriculture alone, and subjected by the loss of a single crop of one article of food to such scenes of national consternation, famine and death, as occurred in 1847.

Paradoxical as it may seem, I believe *the Potato blight* will, under an all wise providence, effect the regeneration of Ireland. Irishmen can no longer depend upon being able to live almost without labor. The root that supplied their nominal wants, and to which they trusted,

'Till scourged by famine from a smiling Land

The mournful peasant leads his humble band',[79]
is taken away, and, happily, while their necessities call upon them for greater exertion, the reward for labor is proportionately increased.

Middlemen, those locusts on Ireland's vitality, are being swept away. The Incumbered Estates Court has brought in a solvent territorial Proprietory to improve the soil and employ the people. Nearly 2,000,000 acres have changed hands since the 1st Sale in Feby. 1850, representing a capital of £15,000,000, and as ⅔ rds of this sum consists of purchases *at* and *under* £2,000 each, a new *middle class* has thus been introduced into the country, and the problem relative to the self supporting plantation scheme of Sir Robert Peel is about to be solved.

The famine of 1847,—which caused £8,000,000 to be expended in opening the arteries of internal intercourse in Ireland, and the sufferings of the Irish people, attracted the eyes of all Europe to their shores, and the sympathy of the Queen upon the throne to that of her humblest subject, gathered around them.

While this was the effect on the *social* condition of Ireland, let us see what it has done for her *material* prosperity:

81

In 1847, the separate Holdings in Ireland
numbered ——————————————— 730,149
In 1851, they were ————————— 618,166

Being a decrease arising from ⎫
consolidation of————— ⎬ ———— 122,083
                        ⎭

[V.]   acres
In 1847, the cultivated land amounted to— 5,238,575
In 1851, to——————————————— 5,658,951

Being a increase of——————— 620,376

During the same period the cultivation of wheat and other
grain Crops decreased as under:—

	acres		Qrs	Bush.
1847—Cultivated	3,313,579	produce	16,248,934	= 398 p.acre
1851——do.——	3,099,401	—do.—	14,184,066	= 37—do.—
Decrease	214,178		2,064,868	= 2—do.—

And I consider *this* change more indicative of *improved agriculture* than if an increase in the cultivation of these crops had
taken place.

The foundation of all good husbandry being green crops,
the next return will show a striking advance:—

	acres		Tons	Tons
In 1847, there was ⎫ in Green crops ⎬	727,738	Producing	8,785,144	= 12 p.acre
In 1851——do.——	1,352,315	—do.—	11,582,324	= 9¼—do.
Increase	624,577		2,797,180	

In Flax the result is as satisfactory,—

	Cwt	acres	cwt
1847 Produced	349,872 from	58,312	= 6 per acre.
1851 —do—	677,220–do.	140,536	= 4¾—do.–
Increase:	327,348	82,224	

(And yet we continue to pay to Russian and Continental Flax growers, £4,000,000 a year for their Flax Linseed and cake.

In 1841— 250,000 Flax Spindles were at work,

In 1851— 500,000————"————————"————————)

[V.] This *increased* area of *Tillage* would lead us naturally to infer that Stock must, in a relative proportion have *decreased*, but the reverse is the case: The number of animals, and their value, was,—

In 1847,————6,248,466	worth	£24,825,547
In 1851,————6,954,739	—"—	£27,737,393
Increase	706,273	£2,911,846

[The returns also show the Consolidation of Farms going on, thus:—

In 1841, the value of stock on } £10,478,484
Holdings under 15 Acres, was }

In 1851,————do.————do.————————4,528,677

decrease———————— £5,949,809

In 1841, on Holdings over 15 acres——— £10,627,324

—1851————do.————————do.——— £23,208,716

£12,581,392

The exports of the *necessaries of life* are yearly lessening, shewing a greater ability *to consume them at home*, thus,

	qrs.
The wheat exported to England was in 1845—	779,113
in 1846—	393,462
in 1847—	184,022
and so on up to——————— 1851—	95,116

[VI.] The progress of internal improvements, apart from Agriculture, has also been great and rapid:—

In 1839, the length of Railway in Ireland was	6 miles
—1846, ———————————	65 – " –
—1851, ———————————	537 – " –
—1852 ———————————	710 – " –
—1853, ———————————	834 – " –

The Submarine Telegraph has joined Ireland more closely to England,—'Dargan'[80] and National Industry have sprung up, and the Exhibition of Irish industry has been held. Paupers have been turned out of Workhouses to supply the demand for labor—Land has risen in value, and its transfer has been simplified; and the law of Landlord and Tenant is about to be amended, and disputes, as to their respective rights, set at risk.

(If Ireland then has made so much progress, under circumstances apparently so adverse, what may not be accomplished in happier times?) [These rapid strides show her capabilities to be great, and it is fortunate she possesses them, for there are many arrears to be made up, and much yet to do. To judge of this, we must compare her present condition with that of England and Scotland:—]

[VII.] Owing the period now under review,—

In England, the population has risen from 15,770,000 in 1841

to 17,922,768 in 1851

Increase— 1,182,768   7⅓p.Ct.

In Scotland, it has risen from——2,620,114 in 1841

to—— 2,870,734 in 1851

250,600   9½p.Ct.

In Ireland, it has decreased from—8,175,124 in 1841

to—— 6,515,974 in 1851

1,659,150—20¼ p.Ct.

(If tested by population, Ireland in material prosperity, is still far in arrear of England and Scotland. But the great stride she has made during the last five years, affords a reasonable hope that she can accomplish all the sister countries have done.)

[VIII.] Had they been Roman Catholic nations, ruled by a Protestant government, and saddled with an Episcopal Hierarchy; they might have lagged behind, like her: but there comes the question,—Would they have borne the Yoke? had they been constituted as Ireland is,

of 80 p.Ct. Catholics
of 11 p.Ct. Episcopalians
and 9 p.Ct. Presbyterians

would they have loved the Lands they live in, and striven for their welfare and their glory? Ah! No! they would have burst the bonds asunder, and thrown the thraldom to the winds,— as did the proud Scots the Prelacy of James VI, and the hardy

Saxons the popery of James II and become a self regenerated, self relying, self governing people.

But Ireland's greatest Champion exclaimed to his country-men in vain, 'Who would be free, themselves must strike the blow.'[81]

(England has done *her* duty, and her heart is yet with Ireland. The outstretched hand of friendship, and of bounty has long been open to *her grasp, and her acceptance.*)

[IX.] And so the giant alien—Church remains, and thousands own the wrong: but England has poured hoards of treasures into Ireland's lap, to counterpoise the evil, and it has only been when ingratitude for aid in Ireland's darkest hour, and when the fiend-like cry; that 'England's misfortune, was Ireland's opportunity',[82] has been re-echoed through the Land, when foreign aid has been sought and none found base enough to fill so foul a mission,—when remitted boons of millions have been requited by jeering taunts of parsimony and continued mendicancy:—*then*, and *then* only, has England blamed Ireland for her own misfortunes.

[X.] The Roman Catholic Bishops in their evidence before the House of Lords in 1825, tried to escape from this differently by stating that they considered 'the Scriptures the *sure* rule of *faith and morals*, and traditions only true as far as supported by reason and Scripture.'

But compare this with the definition of Protestantism by Dr McGee, then archbishop of Dublin, and mark the difference (how far Popery halts behind it). He said, on the same occasion, '*All* who believe the Scriptures to be the *only* just guide of *faith and practice*, and in *the universal right of private judgement to interpret them*, are, thereby, Protestants.'

[I therefore believe the time is far distant when Englishmen shall voluntarily encompass Roman Catholics with *all* the civil privileges they themselves enjoy,—for we must first be impressed with the belief that we can *add* to their liberties without *the risk* of injuring our own; or of imparing that prized *individual freedom* which the cherished constitution of this country enables us all to enjoy.]

{In 1828 the religious element was excluded from the national schools of Ireland to ensure peace and education within her isolated shores, while we *denied* the boon to England and to Scotland: and while here, in justice I admit that the Roman Catholics who have sat at the Board of Direction, have never sought to introduce any sectarian religious book into these Schools, and that I have no sympathy with Archbishop Whateley in his recent objections to the withdrawal of his religious productions from them,—yet tho' the rising generation was thus being permitted to become educated, the Priests of the people did not always exercise their powers for peace, but allowed turbulence and crime to proceed unheeded in their course, until the hand of Providence prostrated the power for mischief; and mark the change as stated in the Parliamentary returns of 1852,—

The executions in Ireland in 1848 were 28
in 1849——,,——15
in 1850——,,—— 1
in 1851——,,—— 2

In 1851 as compared with 1852
the persons in jail were ⎫   10,967
to   ⎬   7,604
being a decrease of ⎭   3,363

In 1852, the diminution of persons

———————— charged with crime was 7,000 = 28 p.Cent.

The diminution of indictments for murder was 41 p.Cent.

and for offences against property———— 27 p.Cent.
and those counties for which *extra* Police had been solicited
and obtained are now petitioning to have them withdrawn.}
[XI.] Now, turn to America and see what the poor Irish, wea-
ried of fruitless agitation at home, and fleeing from the thraldom of their own Priesthood,—are doing on its free soil to
perpetuate this Church's existence.

According to 'De Toqueville'[83]—himself a Romanist—
there were in the United States in 1833, 1,000,000 Roman
Catholics; in 1852 their number was ascertained to be under
2,000,000 notwithstanding an immigration from Ireland and
Germany during these 18 years of from 2½ to 300,000 souls.
An easy inference can be drawn from this single fact. Its confirmation is to be found in the Romanist Almanac for 1853,
published at Baltimore:—

In 1851 the number is stated at ———— 1,980,000
In 1852———————————— at ———— 2,096,300

being an increase of ——— 116,300

now the natural increase was ———————— 59,400
the arrivals from other countries ———— 247,000

making ———— 306,400
and deducting the actual increase of —— 116,300

we have ———— 190,100

unaccounted for, and therefore lost in the American States

alone, to the See of Rome.

[They constitute, however, $\frac{1}{13}$th of the population of the States, and from frequent indications of their power for turbulence, it is not likely to be a consummation 'devoutly to be wished' by their fellow citizens, that their numbers should more rapidly increase.]

[XII.] In all countries, the spirit of Roman Catholicism is the same, and from it we have no reciprocation, in foreign Lands, of the just rights and liberties we grant to its votaries here. It is constantly aiming covertly at an ulterior end, and *that* the subjugation of all who are not within its pale; and, as I have already shewn, its vague negations on this point, bear a poor comparison with the definitiveness of Protestantism, and the conduct of its communities.

God help the Land when Romanists become dominant and continue Papists. Let its people look to Erin—the Green Isle—the Emerald; that once bright gem, when dropped from the Almighty hand into the surging sea, and *there* behold its native children going forth—a second Exodus, to seek a happier home, leaving their own a finished type of human misery.

{Yes! and a people too, gifted by nature with the most brilliant talents of eloquence and wit. Where is the music of their voices now! echoing in the wild woods of the Squirrel and Raccoon! Where is their playful smile and laughing leer sunk in the furrows of a wrinkled brow, and faded on the sallow, but once sunlit cheek.}

[It may be said a Religious creed has no influence upon material welfare, but so sure as Christians are better men and citizens, than Heathens, so are different grades of Christians, influenced in their citizenship, welfare, and virtue, by the principles of the creed they profess.

Irish indolence at home is as evident to our senses, as is the isolated fact of the industry of the Roman Catholic population of Lombardy; so the one may be caused by the Roman Catholic Religion and the other may exist in spite of it, but place a Protestant Saxon beside a Catholic Celt and as sure as the American Indian gives way to the Celt so will he, on an open field of industry, give way to the Saxon.] But the alliance between Irishmen and indolence is broken, and they may no longer lie fallow on their native soil. Though they *may* continue credulous in belief, they *must* become patient in industry; though they *may* continue greedy of national glory, they *must* become lovers of intense peace; though they *may* continue aliens in their heart, they *must* become English in practice,—then the Anglo-Norman Proprietary which the Revolution of 1688 forced upon an original Irish people may care more for their Land and the famine of 1847,—which completed their subjugation to British rule,—may bear less bitter fruits. Who can look back on that sad year, without a prayer against its second coming,—when more than 5,000 fellow creatures daily took a hasty and untimely last farewell of this fair world, until their numbers exceeded 2,000,000. [Then was more than realized the hard lesson recommended to be inculcated by Archbishop Whateley,[84] '*If you want an Irishman to labor at home, don't intrust him with a piece of bread.*' The lazzaroniism of Irishmen is ended and they are no longer to be found lounging, like Turks or Neapolitans upon the Quays of Constantinople and of Naples, and festering in Idleness on their own land.]

[XIII.] England has ceased to consider improvidence and poverty a key to her sympathy and aid; or that secluded people, such as exist in the Highlands and the fishing villages of Scotland, are no longer interesting, *because* they are willing and well doing. Excess of evil brought by Ireland upon England has cured all this and caused its repression: and all the retribution inflicted in return is simply a deprivation of partial privileges, and an equalization of Taxation; England has still her local poor's rate, but Ireland's no longer comes out of the Imperial treasury; she still pays an Income Tax, but Ireland is no longer exempt. Yet let not the Irish people flee from their native Land; if they are willing to compete with others in industry, a fair field is open to them there, where they may settle down without jealousy or regret, and realize every comfort they merit or desire.

'Tis true, a loud voice from the far West is calling them hence, and that last year upwards of a £1,000,000 of money was remitted home to enable them to join friends there, and that 250,000 people obeyed the call; and *still* the voice of the father and the husband cries 'come'; the voice of the son and the brother cries 'come',—the voice of peace and plenty cries 'come'; and the voice of nature and of God echoes 'come'. England may thus lose the nursery for her Army, and the sinews of many of her great national undertakings; [but the troubled waters of Ireland on which she has so freely poured the balm of her bosom in vain, may become placid and still. The Saxon hand of industry may then make their Land fruitful and peace may reign within their Palaces.] May those who go where duty calls them, go to win real freedom, and extend their arms unchecked in the Land of their adoption, taking with them from every English heart the prayer that has so often greeted me in the land they are leaving—'God save you, kindly.' It may be said—

> 'Ill fares the Land, to hastening ills a prey,
> Where wealth accumulates, and men decay.'[85]

But the strength of a nation is as much in the intelligence and character of its people, as in their numbers. In the Lowlands of Scotland emigration is so regular and systematic as to have become a byeword, and the people at home are prosperous in consequence. In the Highlands and Islands, on the contrary, they increase and multiply and remain stationary until overtaken by periodical famine and death, as in Ireland. People must be prudent and industrious to be desirable and prosperous; *then* I will admit 'the might that slumbers in a peasant's arm', and that, 'Burns' was prophetic when he described the domestic virtues of a peasant's fireside, and said,—

'From scenes like these, a country's greatness springs'.[86]

(The foregoing remarks will indicate, that I attribute many of Ireland's misfortunes to the principles of Ireland's misfortunes to the principles of her dominant Church:) there is no inherent evil in an Irishman's composition, and there is *much* excellence and worth. Then let him seize the present hour to become true to his country and himself; let him not lose the present opportunity to obliterate the past, or else in one short year, and on a foreign shore, he may have to heave the bitter sigh that it cannot be redeemed. Irishmen! 'the fault is in yourselves if you are underlings and content to pale your ancient fame and existence as a people before a saintly dogma or creed the fault. See how Scotland instead of passing into a nonentity,—at the voice of John Knox threw off the trammels of a Priesthood and adopted a religion and Creed that sprung from the genius of her own people! See how she, like Shadrach, Meshach, and Abednego,—went through the fiery ordeal of self regeneration and after this purgation and discipline, arose like a Phoenix from her own ashes, arose and became a nation and a people felt and respected in every civilized quarter of the Globe. See, too, how England maintained her nationality at the landings of 'William of Orange',—and even poor Poland, only 'closed her bright eye, and curb'd her high career,' when hope itself, 'for a season, bade the world farewell,'[87]—and *she* has still her living hopes and aspirations. Hungary, too, has been cast down, but not destroyed; the vital spark, though latent, slumbers in her breast, again to light up, to revivify and reunite a people,—to reconstruct a nation.

Then fading star of Ireland, set not yet, and Erin's sons may circle round thee still. Why should an apt, a witty and warm hearted people, pass away,—and that, before a creed inimical (to self improvement and self reliance)—to their national welfare and their progress—with their own regeneration in their hands, and the power to enable their Country to arise to a long and a glorious morrow.

5 Charing Cross,
{August 23rd 1853}

NOTES

1   This note on the flyleaf of the journal, evidently written by a member of the family, is not quite correct, for a reference on p. 67 indicates that Thomas Colville Scott had at least visited Dublin ten years earlier.

2   Known as Lynch's Castle, this fine town castle in Shop Street is now occupied by the Allied Irish Bank, It is partly of the late fifteenth and early sixteenth century; Galway had a large trade with Spain at that period, and.some architectural details of the windows do indeed have Spanish affinities. The illustration has been copied from an engraving in Mr and Mrs S.C. Hall's well-known guide, *Ireland: its Scenery, Character, &c.*, Vol. III (London 1843).

3   The hotel was built in 1845 when there were high hopes that Galway would become an important transatlantic port. It became the Railway Hotel in 1849 when the Midland and Great Western Railway Co. established its Dublin to Galway line. It is now the Great Southern Hotel.

4   Details of the figures show that Scott's sketch of the 'ancient doorway' is copied from one in the *Handbook to Galway, Connemara, and the Irish Highlands*, ill. Jas. Mahony (London and Dublin 1854).

5   Charles Bianconi's horse-drawn long cars revolutionized travel in Ireland from 1815 onwards. Passengers sat in two rows, back to back, with no shelter from the elements. The service to Clifden must have been inaugurated soon after the completion of the road in about 1834.

6   Most of the central plain of Ireland is underlain by limestone, which also extends for a few miles beyond Lough Corrib into an area just

north-west of Galway. South Connemara is largely granite, and the Galway to Oughterard road lies close to the granite-limestone boundary. A low-lying belt of schists and gneiss crosses central Connemara from Oughterard to Clifden, and the mountainous areas north of this are mainly quartzite.

7 John Robertson, a Scots Presbyterian, leased the Ballynahinch fishery from the Martins in 1839 and started a salmon-canning business at Derryadda West near the mouth of the Ballynahinch River. His fishing lodge nearby had become a hotel by 1850; it is now the Angler's Return guesthouse.

8 The Rev. Alexander Dallas, rector of Wonston in England, founded his Society for Irish Church Missions to the Roman Catholics in 1849, believing that the Famine had been ordained by God to make the Irish 'come out from Rome'. With the backing of local Protestant landlords he established mission schools and churches at Castlekirk, Oughterard and other places near Lough Corrib, and then, with the support of the rector of Clifden, in various west Connemara villages including Roundstone. By 1853 the Catholic clergy were counter-attacking vigorously and Connemara was rife with accusations of idolatry on the one hand and 'souperism', the buying of the souls of the hungry with soup, on the other. The worst of it was over by 1869; most of the temporary convertites had relapsed or emigrated, and the missioners were pursuing the normal tenor of Protestant ministry.

9 The Scots engineer Alexander Nimmo who designed the harbours and laid out the road system of Connemara in the 1820s bought out the lease of the Roundstone area, and sublet plots of land along the road by the harbour for houses to be built on. After his death in 1832 the lease of the new village passed to John Nimmo, who was probably his nephew. The Roman Catholic church was built in about 1832, the Presbyterian kirk (now demolished) in 1840, and the Protestant Episcopalian church in 1843.

10 The monastery at Roundstone was founded by brothers of the Third Order of St Francis from Mountbellew in 1835, as part of Archbishop MacHale's drive to combat the Protestant Bible-readers active in Connemara. The Franciscans ran the primary schools in Roundstone until 1974. The monastery has since been demolished and replaced by a small industrial and crafts park.

11 A bridge was later built at Barnanoraun, but the road across the high boggy ground north-westwards to Ballynakill was never completed, like many other Famine works.

12 A hundred and forty is not a wild overestimate of the number of lakes in the famous Roundstone Bog. Despite some afforestation and turf-cutting it is still the one of the finest tracts of lowland blanket bog in Europe, and home to several rare plant species.

13 Copied from an illustration of 'Twelve Bens Mountains and Lake of Kylemore, from the Road to Clifden', in the *Handbook to Galway, Connemara, and the Irish Highlands.* The Twelve Pins are now more often called the Twelve Bens, both 'pin' and 'ben' being anglicizations of the Irish *beann*, peak.

14 Frederick Twining, a young London engineer, of the famous tea-importing family, acquired the 900-acre Cleggan farm (one of the very few portions of the Martin Estate to find a buyer), in about 1850, and later built a fine house on it which is still occupied by his descendants.

15 It is possible to walk or drive into Omey Island over the sands when the tide is low.

16 The beaches at the head of Mannin Bay and at a few places in south Connemara are largely composed of little twig-like fragments popularly supposed to be of coral. In fact they are the detritus of two species of seaweed growing offshore, which have their fronds stiffened by a limy secretion.

17 The Geoghegans, later known as the O'Neills, who had been transplanted into this south-western corner of Connemara by the Cromwellians, bankrupted themselves in turning their house into a Gothic mansion in the 1830s. Part of the unfinished mansion was used as an auxiliary workhouse during the Famine, as were several other large buildings in Connemara. When the estate was sold off in 1853 Valentine Blake of Towerhill, Mayo, acquired Bunowen Castle, as it was called, but never completed it, and it is now a roofless ruin.

18 The two lighthouses on an island off Slyne Head, one with a revolving and the other with a fixed light, were built in 1836. Since 1898 just one of them has been in use. This point is not in fact quite as far west as parts of Kerry.

19 Copied from the Halls' *Ireland.*

20 The sand of Dog's Bay at Gorteen is virtually unique in the Northern Hemisphere in being largely composed of the limy shells of Foraminifera, single-celled sea-creatures. The blown sand makes the grass of the dune system backing the beach very nutritious, and so its grazing was known as a cure for the 'cripple', a condition of cattle due to the poor, wet pasturage of acidic, boggy, land.

21 The rocky mountain is Errisbeg Hill near Roundstone. Scott's botani-

cal list is an odd mixture, and is perhaps the result of hasty reading and unskilled observation. The species now called Irish Heath is *Erica erigena*, identified for the first time on this hill in 1830, a discovery which attracted the attention of botanists to the area; however, Colville Scott is more likely referring to the strikingly large-flowered heather, rare outside of Connemara, *Erica daboecia*, which is called Irish Heath in *Letters from the Irish Highlands of Connemara*, by members of the Blake family (London 1825, republished Clifden 1995). Tormentil is a common flower of rough pasture. *Gentiana (verna)* is a limestone-loving alpine plant well known from the Burren in Co. Clare but not found in Connemara; perhaps Scott was thinking of *Gentianella campestris*, the Field Gentian, which is not uncommon here. *Erica limeria* must be an error for *Erica cineria*, the common Bell Heather. *Adiantum capillis-veneris*, the Maidenhair Fern, has been recorded since 1836 as growing on one boulder far out in Roundstone bog, but it is virtually certain Colville Scott did not see it. A dwarf subspecies of the Juniper is fairly common on the hill.

22 The incorrect derivation of 'Connemara' from *cuan na mara*, the bay of the sea, is repeated in many nineteenth-century accounts; see the introduction for the true derivation.

23 Edward Young, *Night Thoughts* (1742–5).

24 *Hamlet.*

25 The cottage (but not the figures) seesm to be copied from an illustration referring to Leitrim in Mr and Mrs Halls' *Ireland*.

26 The tower (of which little remains today) on Cuilleen Hill near Carna, was one of a chain of signal towers built around the coasts of Ireland in about 1815, when a Napoleonic invasion was feared.

27 No source for this quote although the 'ribb'd sea sand' seems to have been borrowed from *A Rime of the Ancient Mariner* by S.T. Coleridge.

28 Copied from an illustration to the chapter on Leitrim in the Halls' *Ireland.*

29 Copied from the Hall's *Ireland.*

30 The word is Irish, *bádóir*, boatman.

31 A slightly garbled quotation from the *Tempest.*

32 A small Dominican monastery was founded at Toombeola in about 1427 under the patronage of the O'Flahertys. It was deserted by Elizabethan times, when it is said its stones were taken to build the O'Flaherty castle on the island at Ballynahinch. The dramatic details of this piece of folk history given by Scott do not appear to have been recorded elsewhere.

33 Under the Poor Relief (Ireland) Act of 1838, the country was divided into a hundred and thirty areas called Unions, each with its workhouse.

Poor relief was to be administered solely 'indoors', *i.e.* in the workhouse, which was overseen by a Board of Guardians consisting of the local Justices of the Peace and representatives elected by the ratepayers, usually from among the gentry. The system was financed by the Poor Law Rate levied on the landowners and tenants of each Union. Small tenants could arrange for their landlord to pay their rate, and large ratepayers had extra votes in the elections for the Board. This scheme, basically modelled on that obtaining in England and designed for the support of small numbers of paupers, proved disastrously unsuited to rural areas long reduced to subsistence level or below.

34   'Mr Johns' would be Samuel Jones J.P. of Ardbear House near Clifden, who had come into Connemara as Nimmo's assistant, acquired some land and opened a copper mine between Ballynahinch and Clifden. 'Paul Hildibrandt'—perhaps Henry Hildebrandt is meant; he was Lord Sligo's agent on the island of Inishbofin, part of the Clifden Union, and had land in Ballynakill in the north-west of Connemara. Another Hildebrandt, George, contributed £60 to prevent the closure of Westport workhouse in 1846; he was also associated with Lord Sligo, who resided at Westport House. (Dirk Hatteraick is the Dutch smuggler captain in Sir Walter Scott's *Guy Mannering*, published 1815.)

35   This is Inishturk off Mayo, not the smaller island of the same name off the Connemara coast near Clifden.

36   Robert Keeley (1793–1869), actor-manager at the Lyceum in London, well known as a comedian for his 'expression of semi-idiocy or rustic wonderment'.

37   Robert Burns, 'The Banks o' Doon' (1792).

38   Maam Hotel (now Keane's Bar) was built by Nimmo in about 1823 as his headquarters while laying out the roads of Connemara, and after his death became a hotel under his former servant, O'Rourke.

39   Spencer Horatio Walpole (1806–98) was Home Secretary in 1852 and again in 1858–9.

40   Lord Leitrim, far from being 'a good and sensible landlord', was regarded as a tyrannical maniac. He became notorious a couple of years after Scott's visit for ordering his tenantry to occupy all the rooms at the Maam Inn, so that the Lord Lieutenant, journeying through the region, had to travel on through the night to Cong. Lord Leitrim was murdered on his way to an eviction on his Donegal estate in 1878.

41   Most visitors to the Joyce Country on these north-eastern bounds of Connemara called on Big Jack Joyce, who leased and sublet large tracts of land, as had his father Big Ned before him. His house was later

enlarged into a hotel, and is now the Leenane Inn.

42 The reference is most likely to Captain J.B. Blake of Doon House south of Maam, mentioned further on. The Encumbered Estates Court was set up under the Encumbered Estates Act of 1849, to facilitate the sale of the many estates bankrupted by the Famine; over the succeeding years nearly a quarter of the land of Ireland was thus transfered from the impecunious traditional landlords to new owners, some of them mere speculators, and some with capital to invest in improvements

43 James Beattie (1735–83), a Scot, best known for his poem *The Minstrel*.

44 These mountains immediately south of Leenaun are in fact of Ordovician and Silurian sedimentary rocks.

45 'Benbeola' represents the Irish name of the Twelve Bens, Na Beanna Beola, the peaks of Beola, who was a giant of old. The highest peak among them is Binn Bhán, at 2395 ft. The pass of Gleninagh is at just over 1300 ft. At the time of Colville Scott's visit the present road through the Inagh Valley from Recess did not exist.

46 Trinity College, Dublin, was granted much land in the Inagh and Maam valleys confiscated from the O'Flahertys by the Cromwellian regime in the 1850s, and held it down to the beginning of this century. They sublet mainly to Joyces.

47 Dean Mahon of Westport built a cottage at Garroman in 1833 on land leased from the Martins. ('O'McMahon' is an absurdity of Colville Scott's.) After the Dean's death in about 1850 the lease was acquired by a John J. Strutzer. Later the enlarged cottage became a shooting lodge for the Berridges of Ballynahinch, and then in the 1930s and '40s it was a fishing hotel. While the house has been demolished, the woods of Garroman, originating from the Dean's and Strutzer's plantings, are still notable in the bare Connemara landscape.

48 The Irvingites were followers of the teaching of E. Irving, a minister of the Church of Scotland who died in 1834; they called themselves the Catholic Apostolic Church. The Rowanites evidently were some similar sect who proved their faith by miracle-working, but seem to have left even fewer footprints on the waters of history.

49 This encounter with the chimneysweep must have taken place in Rosmuck; the chapel, at the south-eastern end of the peninsula, had been built in 1844, and at that time the priest lived in part of it. (The Maude family still live in Cill Bhriocáin or Kilbrickan, in Rosmuck.)

50 A stirk is a yearling heifer or bullock.

51 Oughterard was not part of the Martin estate; some of it belonged to George O'Flaherty, a descendant of the old O'Flaherty chiefs of Augh-

nanure Castle, living in nearby Lemonfield, and the rest to the St Georges (formerly the Frenches) of Tyrone House in south Galway. Mr O'Flaherty, the postmaster, claimed to be the representative of the Moycullen branch of the O'Flaherty clan.

52 Clareville, at Claremount on the outskirts of Oughterard, was built by Humanity Dick's father Robert Martin, and in the 1850s belonged to a Richard Martin.

53 The black 'marble' is in fact an unmetamorphosed limestone that takes a good polish; it was quarried in a few places around Galway, and its decorative use can be seen in the modern cathedral there.

54 'Jumpers' was an insulting term for Protestants. It seems to have originated as the name of a Welsh methodist sect who jumped as part of their acts of worship.

55 Henry Hodgson's mine in Teernakill South near Maam was producing copper, some pyrites and nickel in the 1850s. The ruins of the mineworkers' quarters and the bed of the light railway carrying the ore to the lake shore can still be seen. Hodgson also owned mines in Wicklow.

56 'Col. Archer' here must be an error for Col. Clements, Lord Leitrim's cousin and later his heir. He owned the lead mine in Carrowgarriff near Maam, which was briefly operative again in 1908. The Dallas school of Castlekirk, a little farther to the south east, was actually on the estate and under the patronage of Captain J.B. Blake of nearby Doon House, the owner of the boat mentioned.

57 'Lough' is the usual anglicization of loch, the word for 'lake' in both Irish and Scots Gaelic, which is a dialect of Irish. 'Pin' and 'Ben' both anglicise binn or beann, peak. Laigh is a common word ending, not connected with 'low'.

58 This is probably the medieval chapel of St Cummin, from which the parish is called Kilcummin, in the graveyard by the main road ¾ mile south east of Oughterard.

59 Shale beds, in fact, separating strata of limestone.

60 Porridgetown has no Scottish connections; the Irish name is Cnoc Bhracháin, i.e. 'porridge-hill'.

61 Kylemore, four miles west of Oughterard, is an area of crag with extensive flat sheets of bare bedrock of the type well known in the Burren and very descriptively termed 'limestone pavement'. There are also many erratic boulders deposited when the glaciers that carried them melted back at the end of the last Ice Age. Neither the limestone sheets nor the erratics were 'floatal', and the limestone pavement is not detached from its substrate.

62 The first Baron Campbell, a Scotsman, became Lord High Chancellor of Ireland in 1841 and acquired his Galway estate through the Encumbered Estates Court after the Famine. His seat was Moycullen House.

63 Galway was known as the City of the Tribes from the fourteen eminent merchant families of Norman origin that dominated its history. The 'Tribes' included the Martins, Lynches, Blakes and others who later became landlords in Connemara.

64 The Peep o' Day Boys were Protestant rural gangs who terrorized the Catholics of the Armagh area in the late eighteenth century.

65 Tonabrocky is from the Irish name Tóin an Bhrocaigh, the end place of the badger sett. Tóin is a common placename element meaning bottom or back portion, and has no connection with 'town'.

66 The Burkes were in fact the descendants of the Norman de Burcas.

67 Bushy Park was the home of Humanity Dick's elder half-brother Robert and his wife, from 1806.

68 Dangan was built by Nimble Dick Martin in the late seventeenth century, and his great-grandson Humanity Dick was born there in 1754. (A 'driver' is a bailiff, one who drives off sequestrated cattle.)

69 Thomas Skilling was Professor of Agriculture at Queen's College Galway from 1849 to his death in 1865, and ran a model farm at Ardfry, a few miles west of Galway city. John Joseph Mechi (1802–80) had a model farm in Essex that thrived famously on very unpromising land; his publications include *Letters on Agriculture* (1844).

70 A Parliamentary bill of 1845 established the non-denominational Queen's University of Ireland, with colleges in Galway, Cork and Belfast. Students were few at first as the Catholic bishops condemned them as 'Godless colleges'. Queen's College Galway is now University College Galway.

71 In eighteenth-century Galway's turbulent election campaigns, a candidate who could not fight duels, ride to hounds over the high stone walls of the countryside, drink deep and treat the voters lavishly, was said to be 'not the man for Galway'.

72 For Samuel Jones see p. 37 and note 34.

73 Samuel Johnson, 'The Vanity of Human Wishes' (1749)

74 'Milesian', from Míl, the mythological ancestor of the Irish.

75 Contemporary propaganda inflated this figure to 400,000; a modern estimate is 4000, not counting those who died as refugees (R.F. Foster, *Modern Ireland, 1600–1972*).

76 Arthur Young (agriculturalist and traveller, 1741–1820); his *Tour in Ireland*, published in 1780, unfortunately does not broach Connemara.

77 Edward Wakefield, *An Account of Ireland* (London 1812).

78 John Ramsey McCullough (1789–1864), Scots statistician and political economist, was a dogmatic exponent of the case for free trade. His works include *Principals of Political Economy* (Edinburgh 1825).

79 Oliver Goldsmith, 'The Deserted Village' (1770).

80 The engineer William Dargan organized the Irish Industrial Exhibition in 1853.

81 Lord Byron, 'Childe Harold's Pilgrimage' (1812–18).

82 'England's difficulty is Ireland's opportunity,' a saying attributed to Daniel O'Connell.

83 Alexis de Tocqueville, *Democracy in America* (1835).

84 Richard Whately, Church of Ireland Archbishop of Dublin, chaired the Royal Commision of Enquiry into the Conditions of the Poorer Classes in Ireland (first report, 1835).

85 Goldsmith, 'The Deserted Village'.

86 'From scenes like these old Scotia's grandeur springs,' from Robert Burns' 'The Cotter's Saturday Night' (1786).

87 'Hope, for a season, bade the world farewell,/And Freedom shrieked— as Kosciusko fell!'—from 'Pleasures of Hope', by Thomas Campbell (1777–1844).

Map

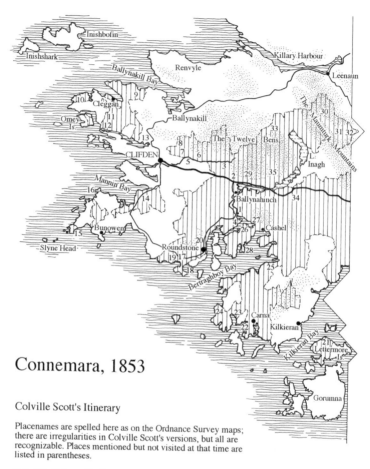

Connemara, 1853

Colville Scott's Itinerary

Placenames are spelled here as on the Ordnance Survey maps;
there are irregularities in Colville Scott's versions, but all are
recognizable. Places mentioned but not visited at that time are
listed in parentheses.

Feb. 5th: Galway; Oughterard; Ballynahinch; (1, Mr. Robertson's hotel and cannery).
Feb. 6th: Roundstone. **Feb. 7th**: 2, Emlaghdauroe; 3, Barnanoraun; (4, Toombeola);
5, Owenglin River; 6, Cregg; 7, Tooraskeheen; 8, Loughauna. **Feb. 8th**: Clifden;
9, Ballynew; 10, Aughrus Beg; Omey Island; 11, Barnahallia; 12, Leagaun;
13, Streamstown. **Feb. 9th**: 14, Derrigimlagh; Bunowen; 15, Ballinaleama; 16, Knock.
Feb. 10th: 17, Errisbeg; 18, Gorteen Bay; 19, Murvey; 20, Letterdife.
Feb. 11th: Kilkieran; 21, Lettercallow. **Feb. 12th**: Carna; 22, chapel (by Mweenish
Bay); 23, Cuilleen; 24, Dooyeher. **Feb. 14th**: 25, Glinsk; (53, Carrowndulla).
Feb. 15th: 26, Derrysillagh; 27, Cloonisle; 4, Toombeola; 28, Canower;
(29, Benlettery). **Feb. 16th**: Clifden. **Feb. 17th**: Ballynahinch. **Feb. 18th**: Maam.

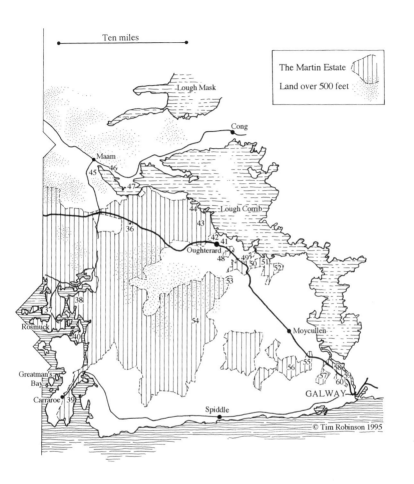

Feb. 19th: 30, Bunnaviskaun; 31, Gowlaunlee; 32, Knockaunbaun.
Feb. 21st: 5, Owenglin River; 33, Gleninagh. **Feb. 22nd**: 34, Garroman.
Feb. 23rd, 35, Glencoaghan; 36, Halfway House. **Feb. 24th**: 37, Kilbrickan;
(38, Camus); Greatman's Bay; 39, Barraderry. **Feb. 25th**: 40, Muckinishederdauhaulia;
Rosmuck. **Feb. 26th**: Oughterard. **Feb. 27th**: 41, Lemonfield; 42, Claremount.
Feb. 28th: 43, Newvillage; 44, Curraghrevagh; 45, Teernakill South;
(46, Carrowgarriff); (47, Castlekirk and Doon House). **Mar. 1st**: 48, Rushveala;
49, Laghtgannon; 50, Porridgetown; 51, Srue; 52, Kylemore; 53, Carrowndulla.
Mar. 2nd: 54, Finnaun; Moycullen; Galway. **Mar. 3rd**: 55, Aubwee; 56, Pollnaclogha;
57, Tonabrocky; 58, Bushy Park; 59, Dangan; 60, Corribview. **Mar. 4th**: Galway.